x mosaics

Tera Leigh

NORTH LIGHT BOOKS

CINCINNATI, OHIO

www.artistsnetwork.com

about the author

Tera Leigh is an award-winning artist and author. Her work has been published in a wide variety of craft and home décor magazines. This is her third publication for North Light Books. She is the author of *Complete Book of Decorative Painting* and *How to be Creative if You Never Thought You Could*, featured on the "It's Christopher Lowell Show" on the Discovery Network. In the years they were published, both titles were named to the "Top Ten Craft & Hobby Books" list compiled by the American Library Association. Tera is also a columnist for publications such as *PaintWorks*, *Quick & Easy Painting*, *Create & Decorate* and *Artist's Sketchbook*.

She was awarded the prestigious HIA Special Recognition Award for her contribution to the craft industry in 2003 and was one of five women in North America to win the Harlequin Enterprises 2003 "More than Words" competition for her contributions to the community through crafts and the Memory Box Artist Program, Inc., which she founded. To learn more about Tera and her work, visit http://www.teraleigh.com.

Faux Mosaics. Copyright © 2004 by Tera Leigh. Manufactured in China. All rights reserved. No part of this book may be reproduced in any form or by any electronic or mechanical means including information storage and retrieval systems without permission in writing from the publisher, except by a reviewer, who may quote a brief passage in review. Published by North Light Books, an imprint of F+W Publications, Inc., 4700 East Galbraith Road, Cincinnati, Ohio 45236. (800) 289-0963. First edition.

08 07 06 05 04   5 4 3 2 1

Library of Congress Cataloging-in-Publication Data

For cataloging information, see the Library of Congress web site at www.loc.gov.

Editor: Christine Doyle
Designer: Joanna Detz
Layout Artist: Kathy Gardner
Production Coordinator: Sara Dumford
Photographers: Tim Grondin, Al Parrish and Christine Polomsky
Photo Stylist: Jan Nickum

metric conversion chart

TO CONVERT	TO	MULTIPLY BY
Inches	Centimeters	2.54
Centimeters	Inches	0.4
Feet	Centimeters	30.5
Centimeters	Feet	0.03
Yards	Meters	0.9
Meters	Yards	1.1
Sq. Inches	Sq. Centimeters	6.45
Sq. Centimeters	Sq. Inches	0.16
Sq. Feet	Sq. Meters	0.09
Sq. Meters	Sq. Feet	10.8
Sq. Yards	Sq. Meters	0.8
Sq. Meters	Sq. Yards	1.2
Pounds	Kilograms	0.45
Kilograms	Pounds	2.2
Ounces	Grams	28.4
Grams	Ounces	0.04

dedication

This book is lovingly

dedicated to two fabulous

and inspiring women:

Sally Finnegan

(also known as "Sales Goddess")

of North Light Books and

Anne Generas

at Ranger Industries.

Without their support

and belief in the

faux mosaic technique,

this book would not

have been written.

acknowledgments

Family Life

It isn't easy to live with a workaholic artist with no cooking skills (or at least not many I will admit to having) and a penchant for working until after the sun rises. My husband, Ken Mugrage, deals with it admirably. As always, Ken, "Thank you for not divorcing me yet." You are still my favorite Knight.

When I married Ken, I became part of an amazing family that is remarkably like my own: that is to say, smart, funny and incredibly loving. My parents, Curt and Marie Gemmil, and siblings, Curt Gemmil and Tonya Mills, and their families Dolores and Madison Gemmil, and Bob and Natasha Mills still make me laugh, encourage me when I'm scared and cranky, and always make me proud. Ken's parents Bill and Ellen, and siblings Bill Jr., Deanna, Nicholas, and La Dena Parks consistently amaze me with the way they have opened their arms and accepted me into their family. I could take up pages listing the many other relatives who have touched my life. I hope all my aunts, uncles and cousins know how much I love them and how much their love means to me.

Girl Stuff

Although I don't actually live in the middle of nowhere, you can see it from my house. As a result, most of my friendships have become long distance, which means that a lot of effort goes into keeping them. Realizing that, I know just how blessed I am to have so many special women in my life. Sally, Margie, Carin, Sandy, Anne, Carolyn, MOG, Lorrin, Stephanie, and all the women of the Belle Papier online group: Thank you for being there for me.

For the Boys

T. Allen Morgan and Ken (Wan) Thompson; for over 20 years you have stood by my side and believed in me. I admire and adore you both.

Taking Care of Business

Although none of us knew it at the time, I was very ill when I came to Cincinnati to do the photo shoot for this book. Without being asked, my extremely competent editor, Christine Doyle; photographer extraordinaire, Christine Polomsky; and "Sales Goddess" Sally Finnegan, among others, stepped in to help me behind the scenes. Without their assistance, this book would not have been finished on time, and I owe them a tremendous debt of gratitude. Needing help was a humbling experience for this overachiever. The grace and generosity with which their help was offered is a tribute to the kindness and professionalism of each one of them.

I would also like to thank Rita Rosenkranz of the Rita Rosenkranz Literary Agency for her vision, knowledge and encouragement, all of which led to the contract for this book.

Now More Than Ever

Any speck of talent I possess and everything good I have ever accomplished must be credited to Jesus Christ, my Lord and Savior. Because of His love and faithfulness, I write and create for His glory.

table of contents

introduction

The idea for Faux Mosaics came to me in the innocuous way in which many discoveries are made. After a night of creating tile mosaics in my studio, I came down the next morning to find what I thought was a piece of cut tile on the floor. I reached down to pick up the "tile" and found that it was a small piece of scrap paper I had cut for another project. Looking at the cut piece of paper, which reminded me of a piece of china, a lightbulb went on in my head. Could I use paper to emulate the look of mosaics?

As a professional and hobbyist crafter, my studio is full of scraps from a wide variety of sources. I loved the idea that people who might be intimidated by "real" mosaics could practice on paper. Working with paper, even children could get the look of mosaics without the danger of working with cut tile, glass or china.

Webster's Revised Unabridged Dictionary defines the word faux as: "being an imitation of the genuine article, from the French word fals or false." In order to imitate anything, you have to create a credible likeness of the original. Over the next year I explored products and materials through which I could convincingly re-create the look of mosaics using paper, paint and other products.

First, I tried a "sandstone" product for faux finishing. I took it home and mixed it with paint to a substantially thinner consistency for a textured background. Soon afterwards, I discovered a dimensional glaze product made by Ranger Industries, Inc. I worked on using these products together, and after seeing the technique in action, Ranger agreed to create a "Faux Mosaic" product line to my specifications so crafters don't have to buy expensive faux finishing products or try to mix their own sand into paint.

That journey and the new Ranger products—also called "Faux Mosaics"—led to this book. In it, I show you how to paint and use the Faux Grout product to create a background that emulates grout. I also include a variety of sources for creating faux tile. Be sure to read the tips and notes you find throughout the chapters; they will give you other ideas for faux tile, techniques and hints to make your faux mosaics come to life!

When I first started working with faux mosaics, I thought that "true" mosaic artists might look down their noses at the technique. My sister, Tonya Mills, who has a house full of her own mosaic designs and introduced me to mosaics, was among the technique's first fans. When you see the texture of the Faux Grout in combination with the glaze of the tile, I think you will be equally excited and inspired.

Whether you use faux mosaics as a way to build your confidence toward creating tile or china mosaics, enjoy the simplicity and ease of the technique for itself, or a little bit of both, this book is the very first primer on the technique. I hope you will take what you learn and develop your own ideas because that is where this technique began—as a little piece of paper that sparked a big idea. I hope Faux Mosaics and this book spark some big ideas for you too!

materials

To create the projects in this book you'll need to have a few supplies on hand: some for preparing and finishing the surfaces and some for making the faux mosaics. All, however, are easy to find at your local art and craft store.

Basic Materials

These basic supplies for preparing, painting and finishing will help you complete your projects easily and get the best results.

Paints and Brushes

Acrylic paints come in a wide range of premixed colors and work well on most surfaces that are appropriate for mosaics. Be sure that your surface is clean, prepped and sealed before painting.

When choosing a brush, buy the best you can afford. I like an acrylic/sable blend because the brush is absorbent but also has good "spring" to it (meaning it isn't floppy and is easy to control). In this book, I use Robert Simmons Sapphire brushes, which are available in most art and craft stores. Rinse your brushes with water after each use, and use a brush cleaner to remove residual paint.

Sealer

Sealer is applied before you paint. It equalizes the porosity of your surface, as well as protects the paint from any dirt, sap or products in or on the surface. Follow the directions when using a sealer, and make sure you use a product intended for the surface type.

Varnish

Varnish is applied after painting is complete to protect the paint. Once again, follow the manufacturer's directions and use a product intended for the surface type. I like to use an outdoor varnish for UV protection. The choice of the gloss level (matte, satin or gloss) is a matter of personal taste.

Water Basin

I recommend using a water basin intended for acrylic paints. Most will have a ridged section that allows you to tap the ferrule section of the brush against it to remove paint from the bristles. Separated sections allow you to clean your brush in one area and keep a separate section of clean water for painting.

Paper Towels

For convenience, I like to use paper towels when I paint, but any soft, lint-free cloth will work. You will use the towels to blot your brush, wipe off mistakes and keep your work surface clean.

Palette

I use a gray waxed palette because the contrast of the gray allows me to see the color of most paint easily. For a less-expensive alternative, use a waxed plate, waxed paper taped to cardboard or tin foil wrapped over cardboard.

Materials for Faux Mosaics

Now I'll introduce you to the materials you'll need to create faux mosaics. With this information, you should be able to move easily through the projects in this book—and come up with your own designs and surfaces too.

Surface

One of the best attributes of the faux mosaic technique is that it does not require the strong base traditional mosaics need to hold real grout and tile. Faux grout and faux tile weigh little, and as a result, virtually any surface—from greeting cards, to papier mâché, to wood—can be used as the base for your design. See pages 10–11 for information on how to prepare wood, papier mâché and metal surfaces.

Grout

The simplest way to create the look of faux grout is with paint. If you are new to crafting or if you're working with a child, a light gray painted background is easiest. For this you will need a palette, paintbrush, water bin and paint.

Another painted background is a sponged finish of varying shades of grey, cream and white. For this you will need a palette, sponge, water bin and at least three shades of paint. I like to use a natural sea sponge for maximum texture.

The Tera Leigh line of Faux Mosaic products includes Faux Mosaic Grout that is a combination of a textured base and a white paint that dries to a matte finish. You can create your own textured grout by mixing clean sand with paint or by using a professional faux finishing sandstone-type texture product. These products can be found online or at home improvement stores in the paint department.

You may need to spray or brush a matte varnish over other brands if the background does not dry to a matte finish. The contrast between the matte grout and the glazed tile is part of what makes the faux illusion work.

Tile

Faux tile can be made from virtually any bleed-proof or nonsmear paper. For this reason, you may not be able to use ink-jet prints because most glue will make the ink smear. However, if you experiment with spray fixatives or matte finish spray paint, you may find that papers that are prone to smear or bleed can be made useful as faux tile.

See the technique section (pages 14–19) to learn how I created the faux tile found in this book. You will find ideas for other faux tile options throughout the book.

Glue

It is very important that the glue used on the tile is thick enough to fasten the paper to a textured surface, and it must dry to a matte finish. If the glue has a sheen, it will make the grout background shiny and ruin the faux effect when the project is finished. If you find that your glue did not dry to a matte finish, spray the project lightly with a matte fixative or clear spray paint after the glue is dry and before you apply the glaze to the tiles.

If, after the glue is dry, you find that parts of the tile have lifted (some papers will want to curl when wetted by the glue), you can paste down the edges with a glue stick. Allow this glue to dry well before you proceed to the glazing stage.

Glaze

The Tera Leigh Faux Mosaic Tile Glaze provides the highest shine and best dimensional finish of any nontoxic glaze product I have found. If you cannot find this product, check craft stores for similar acid-free, nontoxic dimensional glazes in their own applicator bottles. It is important that the glaze has enough body that it will hold its place on your tile. Use an applicator to apply the glaze as brushed-on glaze will flatten the dimensional effect.

basic techniques

Getting your surface ready to mosaic is easy. Just remember to use preparation and varnish products that are made specifically for the surface you are using. Take time to read the labels and follow the instructions. (What a concept!)

Preparing Common Surfaces

Wood

Wood surfaces are readily available at craft stores in a multitude of shapes and sizes. Even better, wood is very forgiving. If you don't like what you've done, just sand it off and start again!

1 | Sand the Wood

Sand the wood with a medium-grit sanding pad, smoothing out any rough spots. For the best results, sand in the direction of the wood grain on flat sections.

2 | Repair Flaws with Wood Filler

Fill in any flaws in the wood with wood filler using a wooden craft stick or a palette knife.

Remove excess wood filler with your finger. Making the filler as smooth as possible when wet will mean less sanding once it's dry.

3 | Sand Again

However smooth you make the filler, you will need to sand it after it is dry to make sure the wood sealer will penetrate the filler. Let the filler dry and sand smooth with a fine-grit sanding pad.

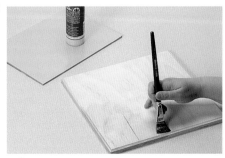

4 | Seal Wood Before Painting

Seal the surface of the wood to seal in sap and dirt before painting. Squeeze sealer onto the palette first and use a large flat brush to apply. I use an outdoor sealer because it is meant to deal with the harshest environments and will protect the wood longer.

Once the sealer is dry, sand again with a fine-grit sanding pad or paper.

Paper and Papier Mâché

Papier mâché does not need any type of prep, except to wipe away any dust or dirt. Because you want complete coverage for the grout, if your paper or papier mâché is not already white, you can use gesso (see tip on this page) as a sealer/basecoat to save time. Otherwise, simply use paint that's the color of your grout as a basecoat, and then begin the grout process.

Metal

Metal must be clean of dirt and oil before you use it as a surface. White vinegar or rubbing alcohol make excellent cleaners for metal because they remove surface oil. If you wet the metal surface with water for any reason, dry it by heating your oven to 350°F (177°C), then turning it off and placing the metal inside with the door slightly ajar. This will evaporate any residual water and keep rust from forming along the seams and other areas where water can hold inside metal. If your piece has rust on it, use naval jelly to clean it, then clean it again with vinegar and dry as indicated. Grout may be applied directly to the metal once it is clean and dry.

Painting Basics

Painting might seem a bit intimidating, but all you really need to create your masterpiece are a few bottles of paint, a brush or two and some cardstock. Faux mosaics are a great place to practice painting because paper is relatively inexpensive, and you only have to use the sections of the design that you like the most when you cut your tile. See right for the best way to load a liner brush.

Varnishing Painted Areas

To protect and highlight sections of the surface that are painted but not part of the mosaic, apply one to three coats of brush-on varnish. I use a gloss varnish to complement the shine of the tile. If your project will be placed outdoors, use a gloss exterior varnish. Never varnish over painted grout areas; the glue will act as a sealer when tiles are applied.

To save time and skip the sealing step, apply gesso to the surface after sanding. Because most craft gessoes have sealer in them, gesso is a shortcut that covers better than white paint. (If you do seal the surface, you can basecoat with paint or gesso.) To apply gesso, use a brush appropriate for the size of your surface. Since gesso is often very thick, wet your brush to loosen the gesso as needed.

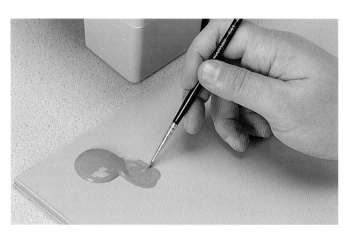

Load a Liner Brush

Place a puddle of paint (FolkArt Light Periwinkle is shown here) on the palette. Before loading the no. 0 liner brush, add water on the palette next to the paint puddle using the brush, then pull paint into the water. Thin the paint approximately 40% so it's thin enough to slide easily off the liner brush.

techniques for faux mosaics

Faux mosaic is a versatile craft because it allows you to practice other types of crafts while creating a new project. For example, try your painting skills on paper, doodle with paint pens or use leftover scrapbook paper from your family album to create your designs. In three easy steps (grout, glue and glaze), you can create a mosaic in minutes, not hours!

Grout Techniques

You can create grout for this technique by simply painting the surface, mixing paint with sand, using sandstone products thinned with paint or using the premixed Faux Mosaic product. What is important is that the surface mimics the texture and color of real grout.

Painted Grout

Painted grout is the easiest of the three grout techniques. Simply basecoat the surface with soft gray, off white or any color you like.

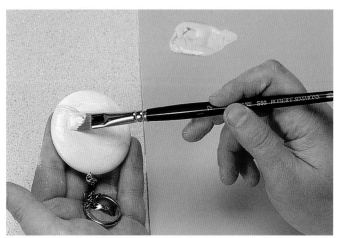

Paint a Grout Background With One Color

With a clean paintbrush, appropriately sized for your surface, paint the background. It is important to cover the surface completely, so more than one coat of paint may be required. Several thin coats of paint are better than one thick layer.

Sponged Grout

Sponging the paint onto the surface allows you to add texture and dimension to the faux grout, giving it a more realistic appearance.

1 | Prepare for Sponging

Traditionally, sponging is done by applying layers of different colored paint to your surface. I like to do this in one step by swirling paint on my palette so that when I dip my sponge into the paint, it picks up several colors of paint at one time. Either technique will work. If you choose to layer the paint, repeat the directions for under step 2 for each paint color.

2 | Apply Paint

Dampen the sponge (see tip below). Dip the sponge several times into the paint on your palette, then press down on your surface. Each time you press the sponge down, turn the sponge a quarter twist in your hand so you don't get a repeat of the sponge design. Cover the entire surface you intend to mosaic with the sponged design. If your paint begins to look too blended and you lose the texture, put fresh paint on your palette, clean your sponge with water then reload the sponge. You can work over areas you are unhappy with once the first coat of paint is dry.

Faux Grout Product

The Tera Leigh Faux Mosaic Faux Grout is applied like paint but it is premixed with texture, so the result is very realistic-looking faux grout!

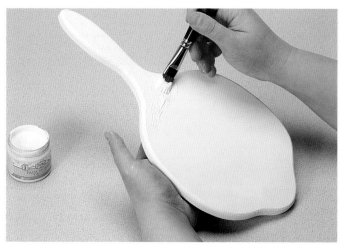

1 | Pick Up Faux Grout With Brush

Faux Mosaic Grout is premixed to the proper consistency. If you are mixing your own, you may have to play with it a bit to find what works best for you. Ideally, it should feel like gritty paint and should be easily spread by a paintbrush. Be sure to use a brush that is appropriate for the size of your surface.

2 | Slip-Slap Grout Onto Surface

Apply the Faux Mosaic Grout using a "slip-slap" motion. To slip-slap, wipe both sides of the brush back and forth to get an uneven texture. For even more texture, bounce the flat side of your dirty (grout filled) brush up and down over the surface before the grout mixture dries.

The test for the correct dampness of the sponge is that if you wipe the sponge on the back of your hand, you should see a sheen but no drops of water should come out of the sponge.

Faux Tile Techniques

Included in this book are tile designs using preprinted scrapbooking paper, prepasted wallpaper designs and antique greeting cards. In addition to preprinted papers, you can make your own designs using a variety of techniques. In this section, I'll show you how to cut realistic-looking tiles, then demonstrate how to make stamped, metal-leaf and simple hand-painted designs.

Cutting Faux Tile

No matter what kind of paper you chose to create your tile, you will need to cut it. When cutting the tiles, make the shapes of the pieces unique. Avoid cutting multiple pieces at the same time or cutting squares, rectangles, triangles or curved edges. To create a convincing faux effect, these pieces should look like actual cut or smashed tile. As a result, you will need to cut through patterns (if emulating smashed tile) or cut out designs in uneven cuts, as you would if using tile nippers on china. Use a wide variety of shapes, some with three, four and five corners, and vary the sizes a bit as well. Keep in mind the size of your surface when cutting the tile.

Cut pieces of tile to size according to the size of your project. Small surfaces will look best covered with smaller pieces of tile. These medium to large size pieces were cut for a larger surface.

Metal-Leaf Tiles

Metal leafing sheets can be used to make beautiful faux tiles, but it's too lightweight to use as is. Cardstock is the best backer for any lightweight design paper. Because leafing sometimes lifts in areas, I find that dark-colored papers work best.

Repeat this process using several different shades or types of leafing so you can mix and match your faux tile designs.

1 | Apply Spray Adhesive

Spray an even coat of adhesive size created for leafing products on the cardstock.

2 | Remove Leaf from Booklet

Metal leaf tends to be fragile, so it is packaged in "books" with tissue paper between each leaf. Regular waxed paper (from your kitchen) can be used to "grab" the leafing from the tissue. Simply press the waxed paper over a leaf and it should lift out of the book. The heat from your hands as you press down on the sheets makes the waxed paper adhere to the leafing.

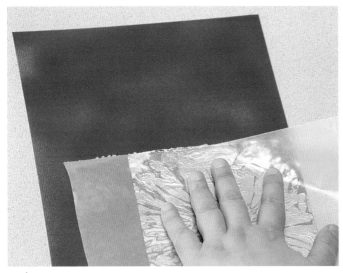

3 | Apply Leaf

Apply the leaf to your surface against the adhesive, smoothing the sheet before lifting the waxed paper.

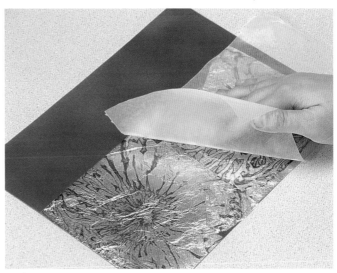

4 | Remove Waxed Paper

Lift the waxed paper away gently so as not to tear the leafing. If any part of the leaf is still on the waxed paper, press down again. If your waxed paper becomes tacky from the adhesive, cut a new piece and continue.

5 | Burnish Leafing

Once the cardstock is covered with leafing, use a crumpled sheet of tissue from the leafing book to burnish the leafing into place and increase its shine. Doing so also removes any loose edges or overlapped areas of leafing.

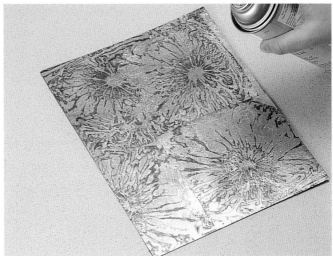

6 | Varnish Leafing

Because this is real metal leaf, spray seal the surface to prevent tarnishing. Make sure to do this in a well ventilated area, following the directions on the spray can.

Creating Hand-Stamped Tile Papers

Some of the projects in this book are stamped with metallic paints on medium and dark shades of cardstock for contrast. You can also use dye ink or pigment ink set with heated embossing powder to create stamped designs on cardstock.

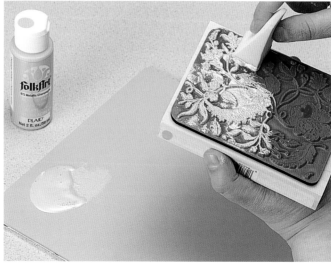

1 | Place Paint on Palette

Pour a puddle of paint on your palette (I used FolkArt Champagne). To load the stamp, press a cosmetic sponge into the paint several times to fill the end of the sponge, but not so much that there are puddles on the sponge.

2 | Apply Paint to Stamp

Tap the sponge onto the stamp, making sure the paint is even without any blotches. Continue to tap over the design to cover the entire surface of the stamp. You can lift paint pooled in between ridges by tapping the sponge over the area again.

3 | Stamp Impression on Paper

Place the stamp onto the paper and press firmly down without rocking the stamp. Carefully lift the stamp directly off the paper to reveal the image. Repeat over the entire sheet of paper.

4 | Create a Variety of Tiles

Using different paints, stamps and colored cardstock, create an assortment of different tiles to be used on your mosaic projects.

Creating Hand-Painted Tiles

Painting the faux tile allows your creativity to really shine. Use your imagination to come up with unique designs. Whether you paint simple dots and plaids or try your hand at vines and rosebuds, you can make your tiles unique to you with a little bit of paint.

Dot Design Sheet

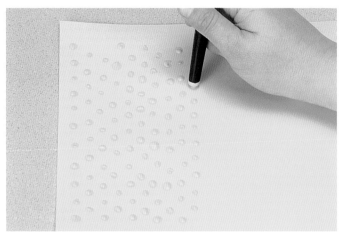

Paint dots on a sheet of cardstock with paint (I used FolkArt Hot Pink) using the handle end of any large brush. Dot the surface twice, then dip the handle in paint and repeat. The second dot will be slightly smaller than the first, adding variation to the design.

Swirl Design Sheet

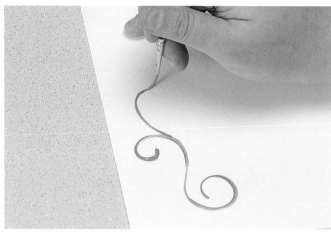

To paint a swirl design, brace the pinky finger of the hand you use to hold your brush on the surface to stabilize your hand, and start by painting a sideways S design. Create the page of swirl designs by chaining each swirl to the next, painting the curve of each swirl in the opposite direction of the previous swirl. A swirl can have more than just one swirl coming off of it so the swirls go in multiple directions. Vary the size of the swirls, making some large and some small, until the section of the paper or entire sheet is completed.

Plaid Design Sheet

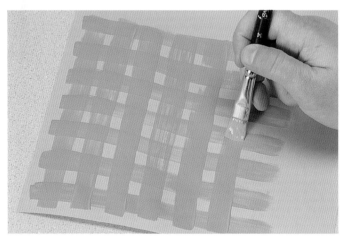

1 | Paint Wide Lines

Using a no. 14 flat brush loaded with paint (I used FolkArt Fresh Foliage), paint horizontal lines on a sheet of cardstock. Don't worry if the lines aren't perfectly straight. Remember that you will be cutting these sheets up into small tile chips, so you can pick and choose the best sections. Paint vertical cross lines in the same way.

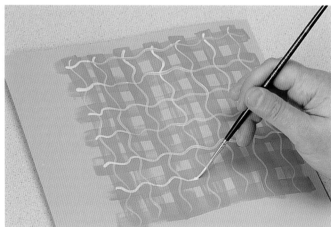

2 | Add Wavy Lines

Using a no. 0 liner loaded with paint (I used FolkArt Sunflower) thinned 40% with water, paint wavy lines down the center of the green lines. Paint all the wavy lines in one direction first, then paint the cross lines.

1 | Paint Swirls

Load a no.1 liner brush with paint (I used FolkArt Fresh Foliage). Paint a series of swirls, as described on page 17, until the sheet, or section of sheet, is filled. These are the vines on which you'll paint leaves.

2 | Load Brush with Two Colors

The leaves on this sheet are "double loaded," meaning that there are two colors of paint on the brush. To do this, lift one color (I used Fresh Foliage) onto one edge of a ½-inch (12mm) filbert brush, then lift the second color (FolkArt Sunflower) onto the opposite corner. It is important to lift the paint from the puddle rather than dipping the brush into the paint in order to control the amount of paint on the brush.

3 | Blend Paint on Brush

Bracing your little finger on the palette, blend the colors by brushing back and forth in one spot. Do not move to multiple spots as doing so will remove paint from the brush. You want to create a small blending area that you can return to as you add paint to your brush.

Add paint several times to your brush to fully load it. You should be able to see the blend of colors on the bristles themselves. Clean the brush when you are finished painting or when you can no longer see distinct colors on each side of the brush.

4 | Begin Leaf

Notice the lines drawn on the sheet of paper. This shows you the one-quarter turn of the brush required to paint this leaf. Start with the brush pushed down flat on the surface (as far as it will go on its side) with the edge of the ferrule (metal section of the brush) parallel to the vertical line.

5 | Complete Leaf

Turn the brush one-quarter turn while lifting it to its tip to paint the leaf. The flat edge of the ferrule is now parallel to the second line. The tip of the bristles completes the point of the leaf.

6 | Paint Leaves

Paint the leaves randomly on the vines, pointing them in different directions. Paint enough leaves to give you some interesting options when you cut the paper into tiles. The sheet need not look perfect; the point is to have lots of vine/leaf sections to use in your mosaic. If you wish, add a stem connecting the leaves to the vines using the no. 1 liner.

Simple Rosebud Design

1 | Load Brush with Two Colors

As you did with the filbert brush when painting the leaves, double load the no. 14 flat brush with two colors (I used FolkArt Sunflower and Hot Pink). For best results, remember to lift the paint from the puddle rather than dipping it.

2 | Blend Paint With a Wiggle

With your hand braced, brush back and forth on the palette to blend the paint on the brush. To get a better blend in the center of the brush, push the brush down and wiggle it back and forth. If your paint skips or you do not have complete coverage as you paint, add more paint to your brush.

3 | Paint Rosebud

The rose is painted in two simple steps. First, start on the chisel edge (or tip) of the brush, with the lightest color of paint toward the top of the flower. Push downward on the brush to the flat of the brush as you move it in the shape of the upside down U, coming back to the chisel or tips as you end the shape. Notice the line drawn at the side of the paper. The chisel edge of your brush should be parallel to that line when you start and stop both sections of the rosebud.

Paint the U shape again, with the lightest color facing toward the top of the flower. Notice that the bottom section starts at the same place the top section started. The lighter edge of the bottom section overlaps the darker edge of the top section without any unpainted section in between the two showing.

4 | Paint Calyx

Use a no. 0 liner loaded with 40% water mixed with paint (I used Fresh Foliage) to paint the calyx around the bottom of the rosebud. This will cover any shaky edges or mistakes. Keep your hand braced so you have maximum control of the liner brush as you paint the calyx leaves.

5 | Paint Design on Paper

Combine the techniques shown above to paint the design on your paper. Use this opportunity to practice your roses—remember, you only need to cut out the roses that you like! Connect the roses to vines with little winding stems coming from the calyxes, using a liner brush and paint thinned with water in the same way you painted the vines.

Gluing Technique

Faux techniques that mimic the real thing as closely as possible create the best effect. Therefore, when gluing, be sure to use a product that has a matte finish so it does not create a gloss over the faux grout.

1 | Glue in Small Sections

This is a decoupage glue technique, which means you will apply glue to the surface, the back of the paper and over the top of the paper once it is in place on the surface. Do this all at one time so the glue does not begin to get tacky or set before the piece is in place. Glue the tiles onto the piece in sections no larger than 3" (8cm) square so the glue does not set faster than you can apply the tiles.

2 | Glue Back of Paper

Apply a thin coat of glue to the back of the paper before placing it on the surface. Because the surface is textured, gluing on both the surface and the paper helps ensure a better bond.

3 | Glue Top of Paper

Finish with a light coat of glue over the top of the piece to bond the paper to the surface, smooth out bubbles beneath the paper and make sure the edges do not curl up.

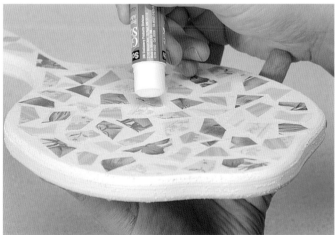

4 | Adhere Loose Edges

After the glue dries, if you find that the edges of any faux tile are not completely adhered to the surface, brush more glue over the tile or use a glue stick to apply glue beneath the paper. Let this glue dry completely before beginning to glaze the tile.

Glazing Technique

Your design will come to life in the final step of glazing. I like to use at least three coats of glaze for a dimensional contrast to the faux grout. Experiment with the glaze to achieve the thickness and overall effect that looks most realistic to you.

If you do not allow the glue and each layer of glaze to dry completely, you may get cracks along the glaze. This can be a very pretty effect, but if it isn't what you want, make sure the glue and glaze are completely dry before you work over them. If you live in a humid area, the glaze may feel dry on the outside but the inside might still be wet. As a rule of thumb, if you experience cracking on the first application of glaze, let all subsequent applications dry as long as possible.

1 | Outline Tile With Glaze

To apply the glaze, first outline the tile, approximately ⅛" (3mm) or less from the edge, using the applicator bottle. As you practice, you will feel more comfortable getting closer to the edge without the glaze pouring off onto the grout. If the glaze does get onto the grout, use a clean and damp paintbrush to remove the glaze from the grout, then immediately reglaze before the initial glaze dries.

2 | Fill in With Glaze

Fill in the center of the tile with glaze (this won't be necessary on small pieces as the outline will fill the entire piece). Air that gets into the glaze causes bubbles. So for best results, put the applicator on the tile and squeeze consistently until the tile is completely glazed, then lift the applicator up and off the tile.

Be sure to study the piece in the light so that you can see any missed spots or bubbles. Don't worry if you miss an edge or small section, you can always add another coat of glaze to fix any errors. Just be sure to let the glaze dry well between each coat before you try to fix any tile.

The glaze will be slightly milky (especially in the center) until dry. You will know it is dry when the glaze is perfectly clear and shiny.

I like to store my bottles of glaze tip down for at least a half hour before I begin glazing so no air remains in the applicator tip. You also can squeeze a bit of glaze out onto a paper towel before tiling to make sure all the air is out of the tip.

If you do get bubbles in the glaze, run the applicator tip through the bubble to pop it, then refill the area with glaze. Be careful not to lift the tip of the applicator out of the glaze as you apply, as this will bring air into the glazed area.

magical
bedroom
mosaics

Mosaics are a hot trend in home décor. From cottage chic to modern, interior designs of all kinds are using mosaics. In this section, we will start out with the simplest of faux tile components: scrapbook paper! Available in a broad range of colors, styles and designs, scrapbook paper is inexpensive and easy to find. If you are a scrapbooker, you probably already have a cache of scraps waiting for the perfect surface. Now you've found it!

Faux Tile

For the projects in this chapter, I used scrapbook papers by Anna Griffin and Tracy Porter. These and many other scrapbook papers come in coordinated designs, so it's easy to select a few papers for these projects.

elegant key chain

This small and simple project is a great place to start your journey into faux mosaics. With a painted background and small tiles, you will be amazed how quickly this project is completed. It is perfect for using up extra scraps of paper and makes a charming gift!

MATERIALS

- key chain fob (Western Woodworks)

- Light Gray acrylic paint (FolkArt)

- scrapbook papers

- no. 12 flat brush

- Tera Leigh Faux Mosaic Tile Adhesive or other matte adhesive

- Tera Leigh Faux Mosaic Tile Glaze or other thick dimensional glaze

- scissors

- palette paper

- water basin

- paper towels

- sealer

To make a random design with your tiles, keep cut tiles in separate piles by design. By picking up a piece from a different pile each time, you will create a more even design. Try not to put like design pieces next to one another, if possible.

1 | Seal and Paint Key Fob

Seal the key chain fob and paint with white paint or gesso. When dry, paint both sides of the fob with Light Gray paint using a no. 12 flat brush. Apply a second coat of Light Gray to the fob for full, even coverage.

2 | Cut Paper and Glue to Surface

Cut the paper into small pieces, appropriate for the size of the surface. (See page 14 for more information on how to cut realistic designs.) With the no. 12 flat brush, apply adhesive to a small section of the surface. Working in a small area allows you to apply the tiles before the adhesive dries.

3 | Use Brush to Pick Up Tiles

With pieces this small, use the corner of your adhesive-filled brush to pick up the tile and place it on your surface. With most tiles you would apply adhesive on the back first, but it is not necessary when the pieces are this tiny.

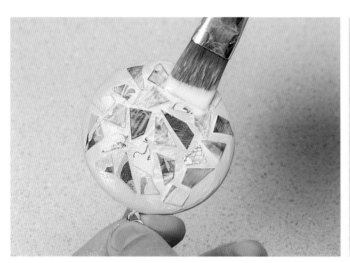

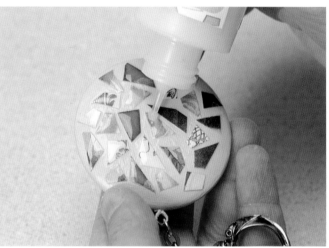

4 | Apply Adhesive Over Tile

Place the tile on the surface, then brush more adhesive over the top of the tile to secure it to the surface.

5 | Glaze Tiles

When the adhesive is completely dry, apply glaze to each tile using the applicator bottle. Take care to keep the glaze on the tile, so the grout remains matte. The contrast between the shiny tile and the matte grout gives the piece a realistic look. Apply three coats of glaze, allowing the glaze to dry to a completely clear finish before applying the next coat.

There is no need to varnish this piece if you choose to apply the mosaic to both sides of the key chain. If not, varnish the back side to protect the paint.

pretty pendant watch

A pendant is an unusual surface for a mosaic, so you will get plenty of attention wearing this unique design! Once again, you will use tiny pieces of faux tile to fit the surface. Although I have used a pastel palette here, you can choose your favorite colors and find paper to match your wardrobe. Simply paint the back and border edge with a complementary color of your choosing.

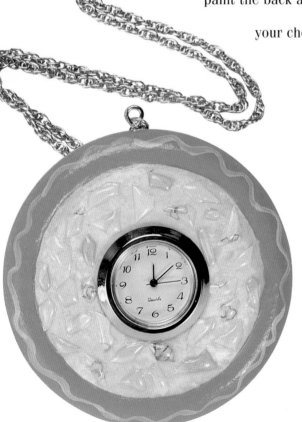

MATERIALS

- pendant watch necklace (Western Woodworks)

- Coastal Blue, Sunflower, Light Gray, Wicker White and Ivory White acrylic paint (FolkArt)

- gesso, optional

- scrapbook papers

- no. 12 flat, no. 20 shader and no. 2 liner brushes

- Tera Leigh Faux Mosaic Tile Adhesive or other matte adhesive

- Tera Leigh Faux Mosaic Tile Glaze or other thick dimensional glaze

- sea sponge

- scissors

- palette

- water basin

- paper towels

- outdoor sealer

- gloss varnish

1 | Prepare Palette

Sand, seal, sand, then basecoat the surface with Wicker White paint or gesso using a no. 12 flat brush (refer to page 10 for information on preparing wood surfaces). Swirl Light Gray and Ivory White paints onto your palette. Dip the sponge into the swirled paint and twist the sponge on the palette. (Refer to pages 12–13 for more detailed information on painting a sponged grout background.)

2 | Press Sponge Onto Surface

Press the sponge onto the pendant to apply the paint. Each time you lift the sponge, turn it (paint side down) in your hand to variegate the design. The harder you push down on the surface, the more subtle the design. The lighter you press, the more the design of the sponge will come through.

3 | Apply Adhesive to Surface

Once the paint has dried, brush adhesive onto a small portion of the pendant with the no. 20 shader brush. Work in a small area so the glue doesn't dry before the tile has been applied.

tip

If you don't have a waxed palette like that shown in step one, waxed paper taped over a piece of cardboard, a waxed paper plate or a piece of smooth plastic will work equally well.

4 | Place Tile on Adhesive

Cut the paper into very small pieces, appropriate to the size of
the project. Pick up the tiny pieces of paper with the edge of your
brush or the tip of your finger. Set the pieces in the glue. With
pieces this small, it's difficult to glue the back of the paper before
setting it on the surface. If you apply enough glue to the surface,
you don't have to worry about gluing the back.

5 | Apply Adhesive Over Tile

With the no. 12 flat, apply glue over the top of each piece as you
place it down to help it to stay on the surface and lay flat.

tip

If the glue is not drying quickly or
remains tacky after several hours,
spray a very light coat of matte fixative or varnish over the glue. Let
the fixative or varnish dry for a few
minutes to set the glue, then continue with the project.

6 | Paint Border

When the adhesive has dried, paint the back and border of the
pendant with Coastal Blue using the no. 12 flat brush. Apply two
coats, if necessary, for full coverage.

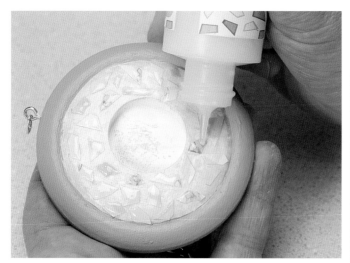

7 | Glaze Tile

When the paint and glue has dried, apply glaze to each tile with the applicator bottle. Take care to keep the glaze on the tile, not on the grout. Apply three coats of glaze, allowing each coat to dry between applications.

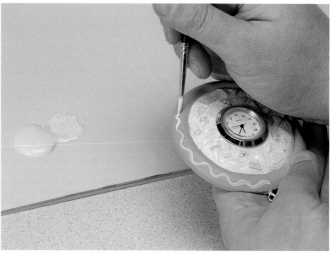

8 | Add Decorative Line to Border

Use a no. 2 liner to add a decorative wavy line to the painted rim with Sunflower paint thinned 40% with water. Be sure to brace your hand so you have complete control of the brush.

9 | Varnish Painted Areas

Using the no. 12 flat brush, varnish the painted wood portions with a gloss varnish to complement the shine of the glaze. Do not varnish the painted grout.

tip

If you are a scrapbooker, you can create faux mosaics with white paper (or sponge the background with paint to add texture), faux tile and glaze. On scrapbook pages, I use a glue stick instead of Faux Mosaic Tile Adhesive because the adhesive will darken the paper and may give it a slight shine.

boudoir hand mirror

Whether you use this for yourself or give it as a gift, a hand mirror is a practical and charming surface for faux mosaics. Because the paper adds little to the weight of the surface, you can mosaic items, like this mirror, that are not normally used for traditional mosaics.

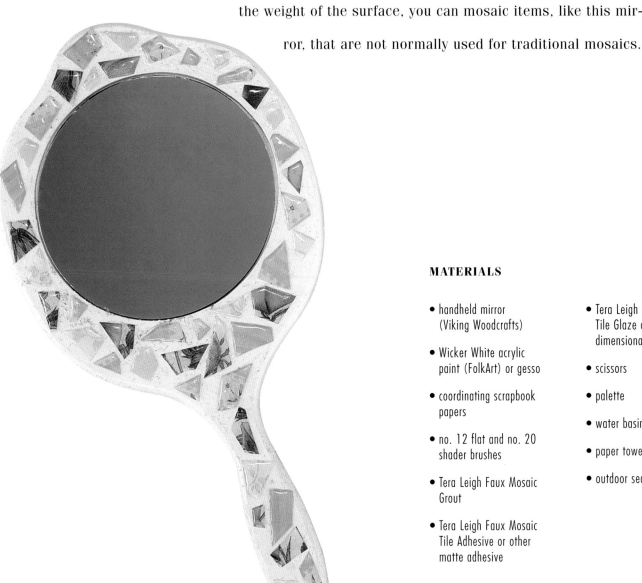

MATERIALS

- handheld mirror (Viking Woodcrafts)

- Wicker White acrylic paint (FolkArt) or gesso

- coordinating scrapbook papers

- no. 12 flat and no. 20 shader brushes

- Tera Leigh Faux Mosaic Grout

- Tera Leigh Faux Mosaic Tile Adhesive or other matte adhesive

- Tera Leigh Faux Mosaic Tile Glaze or other thick dimensional glaze

- scissors

- palette

- water basin

- paper towels

- outdoor sealer

1 | Apply Grout

Prepare wood (as described on page 10) and basecoat with gesso or white paint. Dip the no. 20 shader into the Faux Mosaic Grout and apply it with the slip-slap technique described on page 13. Cover both sides of the wood except the area where the mirror will be glued.

2 | Glue Back of Tile

Cut the paper into tile pieces. Vary the size and angles cut so each piece is unique. Next, brush tile adhesive onto the grout using the no. 20 shader. Work in small areas, no bigger than 3" (8cm) square. Using the same brush, apply adhesive to the back of the paper tiles.

3 | Apply Tile to Surface

Place the tiles on the surface in a random pattern, leaving ¼" (6mm) to ½" (1cm) between each piece. Brush adhesive over the tiles as you place them down to keep them flat and secure. Alternate applying tiles from each of the three papers, and try to avoid placing two like pieces next to each other.

4 | Cover Surface With Tile

Continue to glue the tiles onto the surface. As you get down to the handle, cut a few of the pieces into even smaller pieces so not only single tiles fill in this narrow area. The great thing about working with paper is that you can easily snip a piece to fit.

5 | Fill in Tile With Glaze

Outline the tile with glaze using the applicator bottle. Then fill in the center of the tile. The glaze is self-leveling and spreads slightly, bringing the glaze to the edge of the tile. Continue until all tiles are glazed. Be sure to let the tile on one side completely dry before glazing the opposite side. Apply three coats of glaze to each tile, allowing the glaze to dry to a clear finish before applying the next coat.

stylish jewelry box

This isn't your grandmother's jewelry box! From the striped sides to the gilded edges, this faux mosaic piece makes a charming addition to your bedroom décor. Choose scrapbook papers that complement your color scheme for a practical, eye-catching design.

When deciding how to lay out the painted stripes, make sure every other stripe is a different color and that you don't end up with two of the same color stripes together as you paint around the box. To be sure your placement will work before you begin to paint, write the color name in pencil on each stripe.

MATERIALS

- jewelry box (Viking Woodcrafts)

- wood drawer pull (Hygloss Products)

- Sunflower, Bright Baby Pink and Wicker White acrylic paint (FolkArt)

- gesso, optional

- brass liquid leafing product

- scrapbook papers

- no. 12 flat, ¾-inch (19mm) flat, no. 20 shader and no. 2 liner brushes

- Tera Leigh Faux Mosaic Grout

- Tera Leigh Faux Mosaic Tile Adhesive or other matte adhesive

- Tera Leigh Faux Mosaic Tile Glaze or other thick dimensional glaze

- scissors

- palette

- water basin

- paper towels

- outdoor sealer

- varnish

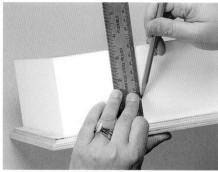

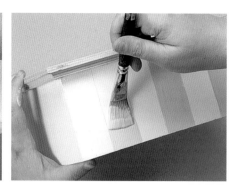

1 | Prepare and Paint Box

Sand and seal the box. Using the ¾-inch (19mm) flat brush, paint the interior of the jewelry box with Sunflower. Paint the sides and top of the box with Wicker White or gesso. For full coverage you may need more than one coat.

2 | Measure Stripes

Measure the length of the side of your box. Figure out how wide to make the stripes by determining the number of stripes you want and dividing the width by that number. I suggest three to four stripes per side. You should have the same number of stripes on each side for a square box. Draw the lines using a ruler and a pencil.

3 | Paint Yellow Stripes

With the ¾-inch (19mm) flat brush, paint every other line around the sides of the box with Sunflower.

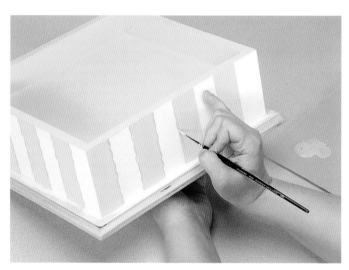

4 | Paint Pink Wavy Lines

Load your liner brush as shown on page 11 by thinning the paint 40% with water. Paint wavy lines of Bright Baby Pink between the stripes. Brace your finger on the side of the box to help control the brush.

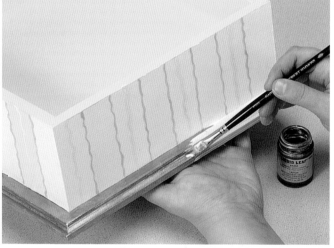

5 | Paint More Lines and Trim

Thin Wicker White 40% with water and use the liner brush to paint a wavy lines down the approximate center of the Sunflower stripes. Don't worry if they're not perfectly centered.

Paint the bottom rim of the box with brass colored liquid leaf. Use the no. 12 flat or any small flat or angular brush the approximate width of the rim to apply the paint. Because this is enamel-based paint, you'll need to use turpentine to clean your brush. If you prefer not to do that, use an old brush that you can throw away when you're done painting the rims or use a cosmetic sponge or cotton swab. You'll paint the top rim after the grout and tile are finished.

6 | Apply Grout to Lid

With a no. 20 shader, apply grout to the top of the lid using the slip-slap technique (see page 13). Set aside to dry.

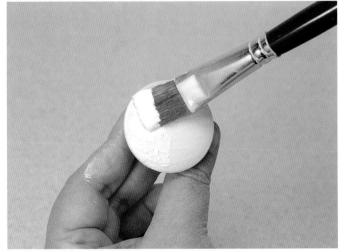

7 | Add Grout to Drawer Pull

Using the same brush, slip-slap a layer of grout on the drawer pull.

8 | Cut Tile

Cut the scrapbook paper into fairly large pieces of tile for the box. Cut smaller pieces for the tile on the drawer pull.

9 | Apply Adhesive to Grout

Brush adhesive onto a small area of the lid with the no. 20 shader. Work in an area no larger than 3" (8cm) square.

10 | Glue Back of Tile

With the same brush, apply adhesive to the back of a tile and place it on the surface. Then brush the adhesive over the top of the tile to secure it to the surface. Continue to glue the tiles until the top of the lid is covered.

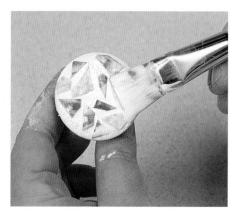

11 | Apply Tile to Drawer Pull

Brush adhesive over the face of the drawer pull and apply the small pieces of tile, as described in step 10.

12 | Outline Tile with Glaze

Run a line of glaze ¹⁄₁₆" to ⅛" (2mm to 3mm) in from the edge on a piece of tile using the applicator bottle.

13 | Fill in Tile with Glaze

Fill in the center of the tile with the glaze. As you fill in the center, the glaze will push down to the actual edge of the tile.

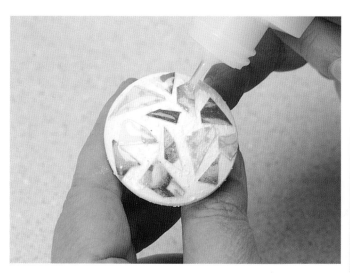

14 | Glaze Drawer Pull

Glaze the tiles on the drawer pull, filling in each of them as you go. Because these pieces are so small, the outline will generally fill in the piece. Apply three coats of glaze, allowing the glaze to dry thoroughly between coats.

15 | Paint Top Rim Gold

Using the same brush you used for the bottom rim, paint the edge of the top lid with liquid leafing. When complete, clean the brush with turpentine or discard.

To finish, varnish the painted parts of the piece with gloss varnish to complement the shine of the tiles.

beautiful bathroom mosaics

When you think of mosaics in the bathroom you probably picture designs on the floors, walls or cabinet tops. Faux mosaics provide a less permanent commitment to your décor, and when you create faux tile with metal leafing, you get a strikingly beautiful design focus. In addition to being perfect for the bathroom, leafed tiles make wonderful gifts for men, as office gifts, and can complement any color scheme.

Faux Tile

The faux tile in these projects is made by laying various metal leaf designs and colors over dark-colored cardstock. Choose at least three colors and/or designs of leafing for each project (see page 14 for detailed instructions). To create the tile used in these projects, you will need the following products:

8^1/$_2$" x 11" (22cm x 28cm) dark-colored cardstock

spray leaf adhesive

metal leaf in various colors and variegated designs

spray sealer

precious metals triangle box

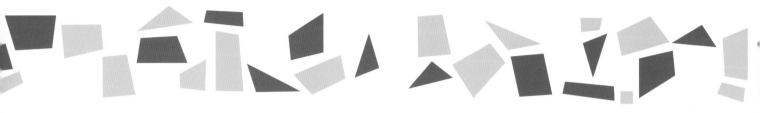

You can transform a simple wooden box into an object of beauty in just a few easy steps. For this project, I have used a plain painted grout background and silver, gold, and bronze leaf tile. The addition of ball feet to the base is a trendy touch.

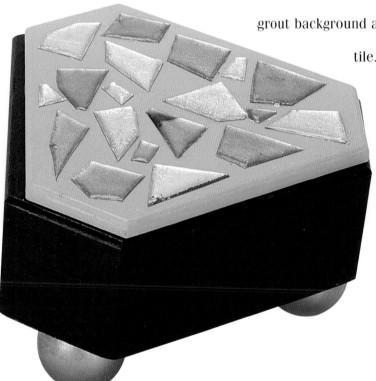

tip

All scissors are not created equally. Tag your new scissors for their intended use (fabric, paper, etc.) and don't use them for anything else. For paper, I like the Kai brand scissors for their excellent blade quality and ergonomic handles.

MATERIALS

- triangle box (Viking Woodcrafts)

- three 1½" (4cm) wood ball knobs (Walnut Hollow)

- Light Gray and Green Forest acrylic paint (FolkArt)

- gesso

- brass liquid leafing product

- gold, bronze and silver metal leaf on cardstock

- no. 12 flat, no. 16 flat and no. 20 shader brushes

- Tera Leigh Faux Mosaic Tile Adhesive or other matte adhesive

- Tera Leigh Faux Mosaic Tile Glaze or other thick dimensional glaze

- scissors

- palette

- water basin

- paper towels

- outdoor sealer

- gloss varnish

1 | Prepare and Paint the Surface

Prepare the wood surface, then paint the lid of the box with gesso using the no. 20 shader brush. Paint the rest of the box, including the underside and inside, with Green Forest paint. Basecoat the wooden balls, to be used as feet, with brass liquid leafing and the no. 12 flat.

2 | Paint Lid for Faux Grout Effect

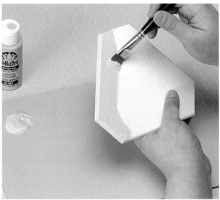

Paint the lid of the box with Light Gray and the no. 16 flat brush to simulate grout.

3 | Cut Tile

Once the leafed pages are dry, you can cut the tile for each design. Avoid squares, triangles, rectangles and curved cuts. Keep the cuts random and uneven to get the most realistic look.

4 | Apply Adhesive and Tile to Lid

Brush adhesive over a portion of the lid. Work in a small area so you can place the tiles before the glue dries. Wipe the back of a tile with glue and place it on the lid in a random pattern. Brush more glue over the top of the tile to secure. Repeat to cover the surface with tiles. For this project, I used tiles made from silver, brass and gold leaf.

5 | Glaze Tiles

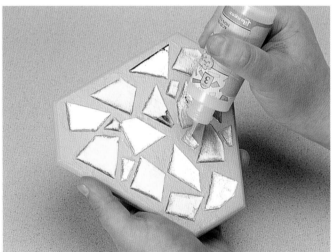

Outline a tile with faux glaze, then fill in the center. Repeat for each tile and let glaze dry completely. Apply a total of three coats of glaze to each tile, letting each coat dry thoroughly. To finish the piece, varnish the painted parts with brush-on gloss varnish. Do not varnish the painted grout.

vintage-look tissue box

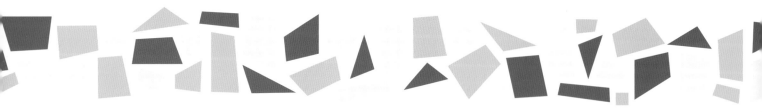

The variegated leaf tiles on this box lend a soft, vintage look, reminiscent of an old mirror that has begun to fade. With a sponged background, this piece is fast and easy to complete. If the green trim does not suit your décor, virtually any color featured in the leaf or any dark color such as black, blue or burgundy will look equally lovely.

MATERIALS

- tissue box (Viking Woodcrafts)

- Light Gray, Wicker White, Ivory White and Green Forest acrylic paint (FolkArt)

- variegated metal leaf in three colors on card-stock

- no. 20 shader brush

- Tera Leigh Faux Mosaic Tile Adhesive or other matte adhesive

- Tera Leigh Faux Mosaic Tile Glaze or other thick dimensional glaze

- scissors

- sea sponge

- palette

- water basin

- paper towels

- outdoor sealer

- gloss varnish

1 | Prepare and Paint Surface

Prepare the surface and paint the front of the box with Wicker White using the no. 20 shader brush. Basecoat the rest of the box, including the underside and inside, with Green Forest.

2 | Sponge Paint Faux Grout

Swirl Wicker White, Ivory White and Light Gray on your palette. Pounce a damp sea sponge in the paint several times, turning it in your hand each time to get a mottled effect. Pounce the sponge on the surface, twisting it one-quarter turn in your hand each time, to get variation in the colors.

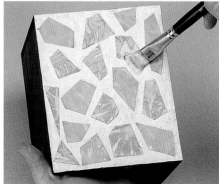

3 | Apply Adhesive

Brush glue onto a small portion of the box, working in an area no bigger than 3" (8cm) square. Continue to work in small areas so you can apply the tile to that area before the glue dries.

4 | Place Tiles

With the no. 20 shader, brush glue on the back of a tile and place it on the adhesive. Brush glue over the tile to secure. Repeat for the rest of the tiles until the surface is covered. For this piece, I used tiles made with three different colors of variegated metal leaf.

5 | Glaze Tiles

Outline a tile with faux glaze with the applicator bottle, then fill in the center. Repeat for each tile and let the glaze dry completely. Apply two additional coats of glaze to each tile, letting each coat dry thoroughly. To finish the piece, varnish all painted parts with brush-on gloss varnish.

lovely soap dispenser cover

Liquid soap has become a staple in our lives, but there is no need to put up with ugly bottles! This soap dispenser cover is both practical and pretty. The variegated leaf tiles lend a sparkling touch to the finished design.

MATERIALS

- liquid soap dispenser cover (Viking Woodcrafts)

- Wicker White and Green Forest acrylic paint (FolkArt)

- gesso, optional

- variegated metal leaf in three colors on card-stock

- no. 20 shader and ¾-inch (19mm) oval wash brushes

- Tera Leigh Faux Mosaic Grout

- Tera Leigh Faux Mosaic Tile Adhesive or other matte adhesive

- Tera Leigh Faux Mosaic Tile Glaze or other thick dimensional glaze

- scissors

- palette

- water basin

- paper towels

- outdoor sealer

- gloss varnish

tip

When laying out the tiles, try to align the edges of the tile piece parallel to the largest piece next to it. This creates a more symmetric flow to your design.

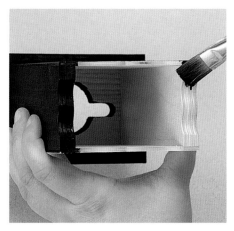

1 | Prepare and Paint Surface

Prepare the surface, then paint the front of the cover with Wicker White or gesso using the no. 20 shader brush. Clean the brush and use it to paint the rest of the box, including the underside and inside, with Green Forest.

2 | Grout Surface

Slip-slap faux grout on the front of the box using the ¾-inch (19mm) oval wash brush. To create the texture of real grout, don't spread the grout too thin.

3 | Apply Adhesive

Brush adhesive onto a small portion of the front of the box.

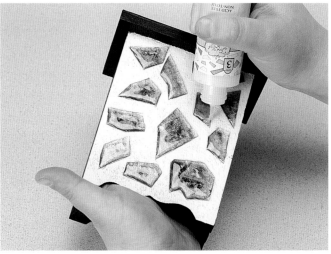

4 | Place Tiles

Brush glue on the back of the tiles and place tiles on the adhesive. Brush adhesive over the top of the tiles to secure. For this piece, I used tiles made with three different variegated leaf colors.

5 | Glaze Tile

Outline a tile with faux glaze using the applicator bottle, then fill in the center. Repeat for each tile and let glaze dry completely. Apply two more coats of glaze to each tile, letting each coat dry thoroughly. To finish the piece, varnish the painted parts with brush-on gloss varnish.

mixed metals leafed tray

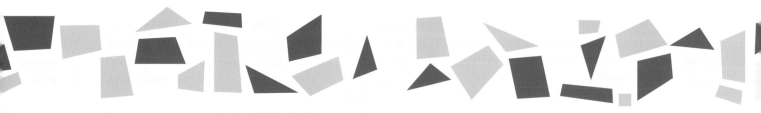

The combination of variegated and solid metal leaf faux tile gives this piece depth and creative chic. Perfect to hold your bottles and bathroom ephemera, this piece would look just as good in the bedroom, living room or kitchen. Because of the versatility of metallics, you can choose a color for the trim to match any décor.

MATERIALS

- tray (Viking Woodcrafts)
- Wicker White and Green Forest acrylic paint (FolkArt)
- gesso, optional
- solid and variegated metal leaf in at least three colors on card-stock
- scissors

- no. 20 shader and ¾-inch (19mm) oval wash brushes
- Tera Leigh Faux Mosaic Grout
- Tera Leigh Faux Mosaic Tile Adhesive or other matte adhesive
- Tera Leigh Faux Mosaic Tile Glaze or other thick dimensional glaze
- palette
- water basin
- paper towels
- outdoor sealer
- gloss varnish

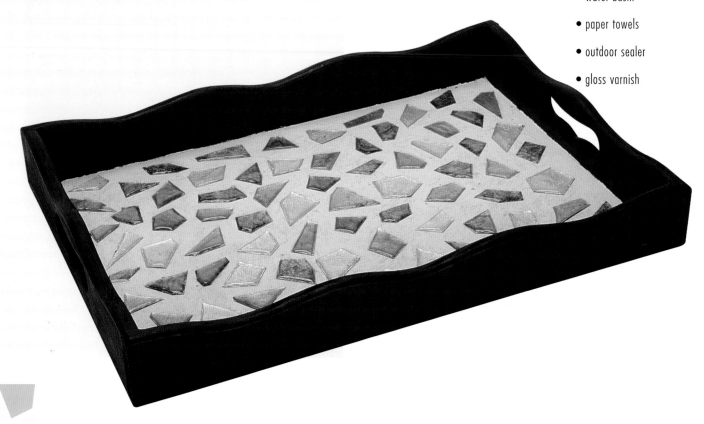

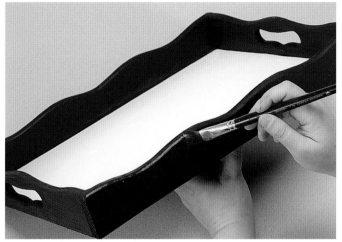

1 | Prepare and Paint Surface

Prepare the surface, then paint the inside bottom of the tray with Wicker White or gesso using the no. 20 shader. Basecoat the rest of the tray, including the sides and bottom, with Green Forest.

2 | Grout Surface

Slip-slap faux grout on the bottom of the tray using the ¾-inch (19mm) oval wash. To maintain the texture of the grout, keep the brush moving and make sure the grout covers the entire center of the tray.

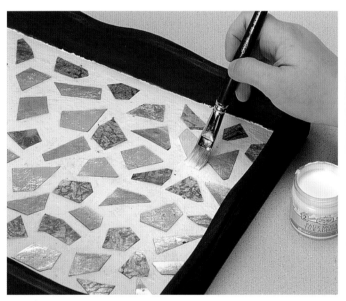

3 | Place Tiles

Brush adhesive onto a small portion of the tray bottom with the no. 20 shader. Work in an area no bigger than 3" (8cm) square so the adhesive doesn't dry before you place the tiles. Wipe the back of a tile with glue and place it on the tray. Brush more glue over the top of the tile to secure. Repeat to cover the surface with tiles. For this project, I used tiles made from silver, gold and variegated leaf.

4 | Glaze Tiles

Outline a tile with faux glaze using the applicator bottle, then fill in the center. Repeat for each tile and let glaze dry completely. Apply two more coats of glaze to each tile, letting each coat dry thoroughly. To finish the piece, varnish the painted trim with brush-on gloss varnish.

divine
dining
room
mosaics

Since the dining room isn't used daily in most homes, one often overlooks its décor. These easy pieces are an inexpensive way to give your dining space a new look. Versatile enough for a party or for everyday décor, you'll love the drama of the black grout, jewel-toned papers and metallic accents.

Faux Tile

The faux tile on these dining room designs is created with rubber stamps and metallic paints over jewel-toned dark papers. You can substitute ink or embossed stamp designs if you wish. See page 16 for directions on how to create stamped tile. To create the tile in this chapter, I used the following materials:

Metallic Solid Bronze, Metallic Antique Gold, Metallic Inca Gold and Metallic Silver Sterling paints (FolkArt)

Anna Griffin All Night Media Background Stamps 580K01, 580K03, 580K02, 580C04 and 580C01

cosmetic sponge

8½" x 11" (22cm x 28cm) dark cardstock

versatile centerpiece box

The gilded center surrounded by black grout is pure drama. This box is extremely versatile, the perfect stage for candles, flowers, pebbles or other visual presentations. Add knob feet for a variation on this design.

MATERIALS

- rectangle box (Viking Woodcrafts)

- sea sponge

- Licorice, Yellow Ochre, Dark Gray, Light Gray, Metallic Inca Gold and Metallic Silver Sterling acrylic paint (FolkArt)

- no. 14 flat and no. 20 shader brushes

- Tera Leigh Faux Mosaic Tile Adhesive or other matte adhesive

- Tera Leigh Faux Mosaic Tile Glaze or other thick dimensional glaze

- scissors

- palette

- water basin

- paper towels

- outdoor sealer

- gloss varnish

1 | Prepare and Paint Surface

Prepare the wood surface, and paint the base piece and the inside of the box with Yellow Ochre using the no. 20 shader brush. Once this is dry, paint over the Yellow Ochre section with Metallic Inca Gold. Paint the sides and rim of the box Licorice.

2 | Prepare Palette for Painted Grout

Swirl the following paints on your palette: Licorice, Dark Gray, Light Gray and Metallic Silver Sterling. Pounce a damp sea sponge in the paint several times, turning it each time to get a mottled effect. (See pages 12-13 for more information on painting a sponged grout background.)

3 | Sponge Grout on Surface

Pounce the sponge on the black portion of the box, twisting it one-quarter turn in your hand each time to get variation in the colors. Periodically pick up more paint from the palette to vary the look of the grout. Let the paint dry completely.

4 | Apply Adhesive

Brush adhesive over a small area of the sponged section with a no. 14 flat brush. Although the glue appears milky over the dark background, it will dry to a clear finish.

5 | Place and Glaze Tiles

Brush glue on the back of a tile, then place it onto the adhesive. Brush glue over the top of the tile to secure. Continue until sponged areas are covered with faux tile. Let dry until adhesive is clear.

Apply three coats of glaze over each tile with the applicator bottle, allowing the glaze to dry completely between coats. Varnish the painted center and trim with gloss varnish.

gilded candleholders

Candles continue to be a hot trend in home décor. These sophisticated candlesticks are perfect for a romantic dinner on your table or to dress up any room of the house. If dark colors don't suit your color scheme, use the white grout you see in other chapters of this book. Choose tile colors to suit your taste.

MATERIALS

- candleholders (Viking Woodcrafts)
- Licorice, Yellow Ochre and Metallic Inca Gold acrylic paint (FolkArt)
- no. 14 flat brush
- Tera Leigh Faux Mosaic Grout
- Tera Leigh Faux Mosaic Tile Adhesive or other matte adhesive
- Tera Leigh Faux Mosaic Tile Glaze or other thick dimensional glaze
- scissors
- palette paper
- water basin
- paper towels
- outdoor sealer
- gloss varnish

1 | Paint and Grout Surface

Prepare the wood surface, then paint the top and bottom pieces with Yellow Ochre. When dry, paint over the same areas with Metallic Inca Gold. The center section of each holder will be grouted, so you may simply seal the area and apply the grout. Slip-slap the grout onto the surface with the no. 14 flat, then paint the grouted area black.

2 | Adhere Tiles

Brush adhesive over a small part of the center area with the no. 14 flat brush. Brush glue on the back of each tile, then place onto the adhesive. Wipe glue over the top of each tile to secure it in place. The adhesive appears very white on the black grout, but it will dry clear.

3 | Place Tiles and Glaze

Continue to place tiles until the grouted center area is covered. For this project, I decided to use only tiles that were stamped with gold paint. Let adhesive dry completely.

Prop the candleholder so the side is level, and glaze over each tile three times using the applicator bottle. Allow the glaze to dry completely between coats. Let each side dry before glazing the next. Varnish the painted trim with gloss varnish.

Stylish Napkin Rings

Napkin rings are a simple way to dress up any table. This dramatic palette is the perfect touch for a special occasion or anytime you want to create a festive atmosphere. Inexpensive and readily available, the napkin rings also make a wonderful hostess gift.

1. Grout and Paint Rings

Prepare the wood napkin rings, then brush grout on the outside of the rings using the slip-slap technique and the no. 14 flat. Allow the grout to dry completely. Paint the grout with Licorice paint.

2. Apply Tiles

Cut small tiles from the stamped paper; for this piece, I used tiles cut from papers stamped with the copper and champagne colored paints. Brush glue onto a small portion of the napkin ring with the no. 14 flat. Place tiles onto the glue and brush over the tile with glue to secure. Place tiles all around the outside of the napkin ring.

3. Glaze Tiles

Glaze each tile three times, allowing glaze to dry thoroughly between coats. Because the surface is curved, glaze a small section at a time. Varnish the inside of the napkin rings with gloss varnish for a smooth finish.

charming chargers

Plate chargers add elegance and drama to your table setting. While they are often expensive in stores, they are relatively inexpensive when purchased unfinished and decorated yourself. With the gold center and the black grout, the chargers are a dramatic foil for any china.

MATERIALS

- wooden plate chargers (Viking Woodcrafts)

- Licorice, Yellow Ochre and Metallic Inca Gold acrylic paint (FolkArt)

- no. 1 and 3/4-inch (19mm) oval wash brushes

- Tera Leigh Faux Mosaic Grout

- Tera Leigh Faux Mosaic Tile Adhesive or other matte adhesive

- Tera Leigh Faux Mosaic Tile Glaze or other thick dimensional glaze

- scissors

- palette

- water basin

- paper towels

- outdoor sealer

- gloss varnish

1 | Prepare Surface

Prep the wood chargers, and paint the center of the plate chargers with Yellow Ochre using the no. 1 oval wash brush. Paint the back and rim of the charger with Licorice. Once the Yellow Ochre is dry, brush a coat of Metallic Inca Gold over it for a gilded sheen. The coverage on the gold does not need to be opaque, just enough to give these areas a bit of shine. Note: If using the Faux Mosaic Grout product, you may simply seal the rims of the chargers instead of painting them black.

2 | Grout Surface

Apply faux grout to the rim and edge of each charger with the ¾-inch (19mm) oval wash brush using the slip-slap technique. Once the grout has dried, paint the rim with Licorice using the ¾-inch (19mm) brush.

3 | Apply Tiles, Glaze and Varnish

Brush adhesive over a small section of the rim. Brush glue on the back of each tile, then place onto the adhesive. Wipe glue over the top of each tile to secure. Let adhesive dry completely.

Glaze over each tile three times with the applicator bottle, allowing the glaze to dry completely between coats. Varnish the center and back of the chargers with gloss varnish.

tip

When choosing faux tiles, choose two or three that complement one another both in color and design. For example, a stripe, a solid and a floral work well together. Three florals, however, might become too busy. Hold the papers together against a white background to see if they match. Whenever I'm not sure, I set the sheets together and walk away, then come back to look at them again later. Sometimes two colors in the papers will clash, and you can't see it until you've had time away.

lively living room mosaics

Assorted painted papers.

Of all the faux tile in this book, the most cus-
tomizable are the hand-painted designs in this
chapter. In the living room pieces shown here
(all of which could easily be used in other
rooms), I have used a bright pastel palette
and some simple mixed pattern designs. You
can take these same techniques, or any other
designs you like to paint, and create a perfect
match for your décor. Use your existing fab-
rics and decorations for inspiration and create
a look that is uniquely yours.

Faux Tile

For the tiles in these projects, I
used painted designs on cardstock as shown on pages 17–19.
Painting a variety of patterns in
an array of colors gave me a lot
of flexiblity in choosing the perfect tiles for each project. Use
the colors of paint and cardstock
that complement your décor or,
to create the tiles as I did, you'll
need the following supplies:

white and light purple cardstock

Fresh Foliage, Baby Pink,
Sunflower acrylic paints (FolkArt)

brushes

wavy-chic frame

Each of the projects in this section dons at least three unique patterns. You can mix and match any of the patterns shown on pages 17–19. You might also use solid-colored cardstock as one of the "patterns" for a bolder color palette. Frames are practical surfaces to work with, and they make great gifts. Creating a custom design with hand-painted tiles makes this frame priceless!

MATERIALS

- scallop frame, 8" x 10" (20cm x 26cm) with a 4" x 6" (10cm x 15cm) opening (Walnut Hollow)

- Wicker White paint (FolkArt)

- gesso, optional

- no. 16 flat and ¾-inch (19mm) oval wash brushes

- Tera Leigh Faux Mosaic Grout

- Tera Leigh Faux Mosaic Tile Adhesive or other matte adhesive

- Tera Leigh Faux Mosaic Tile Glaze or other thick dimensional glaze

- scissors

- palette

- water basin

- paper towels

- outdoor sealer

- gloss or satin varnish

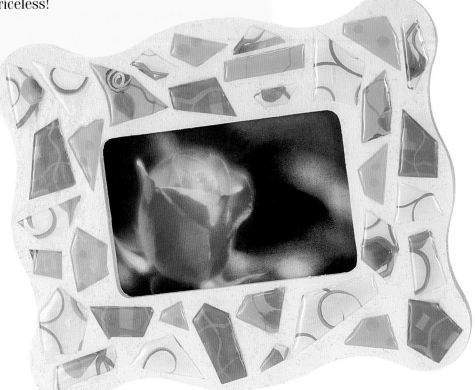

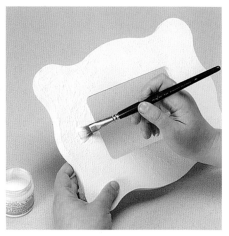

1 | Prepare and Paint Surface

Sand and seal the frame. Paint the entire surface, including the sides and back, with Wicker White or gesso using the ¾-inch (19mm) oval wash brush.

2 | Grout Surface

Using the slip-slap method, apply faux grout to the frame with the ¾-inch (19mm) wash brush. Use both sides of the flat of the brush to make loose X patterns to maintain the texture of the grout. Cover the front and sides of the frame with grout.

3 | Apply Adhesive

Generously brush adhesive onto a small portion of the frame with the no. 16 flat brush. Work in an area no bigger than 3" (8cm) square so you can apply the tiles before the adhesive dries.

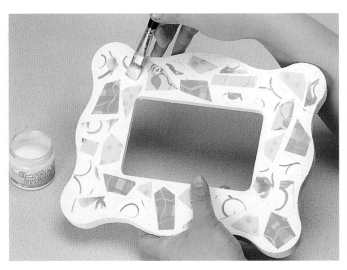

4 | Place Tiles

Brush glue on the back of a tile and place it on the adhesive using the tip of the brush or your fingers. Brush over top of the tile with glue. Continue until the front of the frame is covered in tiles spaced approximately ¼" (6mm) apart. For this project, I selected tiles from six different painted designs.

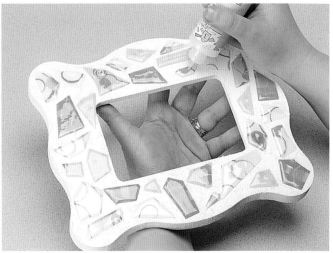

5 | Glaze Tiles

Outline a tile slightly within the edges with glaze, using the applicator bottle, then fill in the center of the tile with glaze. Repeat until all tiles are glazed. Let glaze dry completely, then apply two more coats. Make sure each coat of glaze dries completely to a clear, nontacky, finish before applying the next coat.

It is a good idea to seal the back of the frame with a clear brush-on varnish to protect it from scratches, dirt and damage.

pretty pendulum clock

This surface is a delightful mix of old-fashioned and modern styling. The addition of the faux tile pieces on the face of the clock and the pendulum itself will make it a conversation piece and heirloom for your family. This piece also makes a wonderful gift, as it can be customized for any color theme.

MATERIALS

- small pendulum clock and clockworks (Walnut Hollow)

- Sunflower, Fresh Foliage, Coastal Blue, Baby Pink and Wicker White acrylic paint (FolkArt)

- gesso, optional

- Tera Leigh Faux Mosaic Grout

- Tera Leigh Faux Mosaic Tile Adhesive or other matte adhesive

- Tera Leigh Faux Mosaic Tile Glaze or other thick dimensional glaze

- no. 10 flat, no. 16 flat, ¾-inch (19mm) flat, ¾-inch (19mm) oval wash and 2/0 liner brushes

- scissors

- palette

- water basin

- paper towels

- outdoor sealer

- gloss or satin varnish

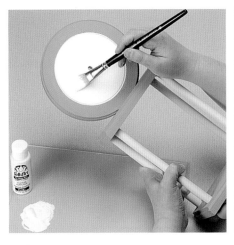 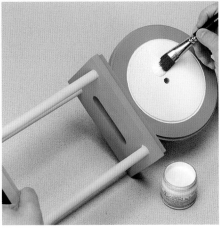 

1 | Prepare and Paint Surface

Sand and seal the clock. Paint the vertical spindles of the base in Sunflower and the rest of the clock, except for the face, in Fresh Foliage. Paint the clock face Wicker White or with gesso. Use brushes appropriate for the size of the area. I used a ¾-inch (19mm) flat and a no. 16 flat for this clock.

2 | Grout Clock Face

Apply grout to the face of the clock using the slip-slap technique. Use the ¾-inch (19mm) oval wash brush to apply the grout so you can easily go around the rounded edges.

3 | Grout Pendulum

Brush grout on the pendulum in the same way with the no. 16 flat brush. The grout will adhere to the metal, just as it does the wood. No additional preparation is necessary.

4 | Place Tiles on Face

Brush adhesive onto a small portion of the face with the no. 16 flat. Work in an area no bigger than 3" (8cm) square so you can apply the tiles before the adhesive dries. Brush glue on the back of a tile and place it on the adhesive. Brush over top of the tile with glue. Continue until the face section of the clock is covered with tiles spaced approximately ¼" (6mm) apart. For this piece, I used tiles painted on three different colored cardstocks for greater contrast against the white grout.

5 | Place Tiles on Pendulum

Cut the tiles very small for the pendulum. Apply adhesive to a small area of the pendulum, then place the tiles on the glue (the pieces may be too tiny to brush glue onto their backs). You may find it easiest to use the corner of your brush to pick up the tiles. Place the tiles approximately ⅛" (3mm) apart to allow the grout to show through. Brush over top of the tiles to secure them as you lay them down onto the surface.

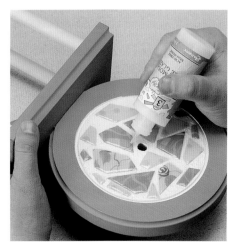

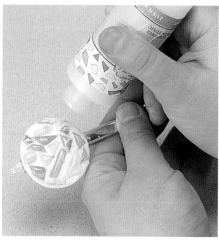

6 | Glaze Tiles on Clock Face

For the larger tiles on the face of the clock, outline a tile slightly within the edges with glaze, using the applicator bottle. Then fill in the center of the tile with glaze. Repeat until all tiles are glazed. Be sure to move the surface under the light as you may miss a tile or find that you have not fully covered the tile in glaze. The reflection of the light will reveal imperfections. Let glaze dry completely. Apply two more coats of glaze, allowing each to dry completely to a clear finish before applying the next. The more coats you apply, the more realistic the tile effect will be.

7 | Glaze Tiles on Pendulum

Since the tiles on the pendulum are so small, carefully fill in each. There's no need to try to outline the tiles first. Apply two more coats of glaze, allowing each to dry completely to a clear finish before applying the next.

8 | Paint Trim

With Sunflower paint thinned 40% with water, use a 2/0 liner to paint a wavy line around the face of the clock. When you paint with a liner, be sure to brace your hand for maximum control. With the handle end of the brush, paint dots in the dips of the waves with Sunflower paint.

When glazing tiles, be sure to clear the applicator tip periodically. If glaze hardens in the tip, it might lift off previous applications as you're glazing. Do not use a brush to apply the glaze as this will flatten its dimensional effect.

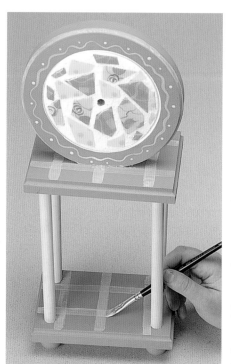

9 | Finish Painting

Paint the bevel around the face of the clock with Sunflower with the no. 16 flat. Paint Coastal Blue along the beveled edge of the top and bottom horizontal pieces with the no. 10 flat. On the top and bottom horizontal sections, drybrush (meaning don't wet your brush, just load it with paint) vertical stripes of Baby Pink with the no. 10 flat brush. Paint horizontal lines with Sunflower. Drybrushing these lines will give them an uneven textured appearance; the paint will have lines and striations in it from the bristles of the brush and texture of the wood. Don't worry about making the lines perfectly straight, but try to keep them evenly spaced. When the paint has dried, varnish the painted parts of the clock and attach the clockworks.

Luscious Tower Lamp

I have looked for a good lamp for crafting projects for a long time, and I like
this one because it's large enough to take a design without being too ornate.
Customize the color palette to match any room in your house!

1. Prepare and Paint Surface

Sand and seal the lamp base. Use a ¾-inch (19mm) oval wash brush
to paint the base of the lamp with Periwinkle, the center area with
Wicker White or gesso, and the top section with Light Periwinkle.

2. Grout Center Section

Apply faux grout to all sides of the center section with the ¾-inch
(19mm) flat brush. Slip-slap the grout on, then let dry completely.

3. Place Tiles

Brush adhesive onto a small portion of the lamp with a no. 16 flat
brush. Brush glue on the back of each tile and place on the adhesive.
Brush over top of each tile with glue. Cover all four sides of the lamp.
For this piece I used tiles painted on white cardstock.

4. Glaze Tiles

Once completely dry, use the applicator bottle to outline each tile with
glaze, then fill in the center of the tile with glaze. Repeat until all tiles
are glazed. Apply two more coats of glaze after each coat has dried
completely. Varnish the trim on the lamp, then assemble the lamp
workings. If your shade is too plain for your tastes, paint a design similar to those in your tiles along its bottom edge.

delightful outdoor mosaics

Wallpaper is growing in popularity again: both the traditional rolls and cutouts. The projects in this section use wallpaper cutouts, but you can use those leftover rolls of paper or border in your closet. You can also ask for discontinued wallpaper books at wallpaper and home improvement stores. Stores aren't allowed to sell them and usually are happy to give them to you for your crafting projects.

Faux Tile

Wallpaper cutouts were used to create the tiles for the projects in this chapter. The fact that some edges of the cutouts will be rounded (because the shapes are round) gives the tile the appearance of having come from the edge of a round plate. If you don't like that look, you can trim the edges to make them straight.

blooming coasters

These ceramic coasters are both practical and decorative.

With the sunflower cutouts, you can bring a bit of floral magic into your garden without planting a thing. They're perfect for your patio, but don't stop there—they also can bring some of the outdoors into your home.

MATERIALS

- coasters (Cridgeware)
- Wicker White, Light Gray and Ivory White acrylic paint (FolkArt)
- sunflower wallpaper cutouts (Wallies pattern #12144)
- no. 12 flat brush
- Tera Leigh Faux Mosaic Tile Adhesive or other matte adhesive
- Tera Leigh Faux Mosaic Tile Glaze or other thick dimensional glaze

- sea sponge
- scissors
- palette
- water basin
- paper towels
- outdoor sealer
- gloss varnish

1 | Prepare Paint on Palette

This surface does not require sealing or basecoating. Grout the coasters with the sponging technique described on pages 12–13. For the painted grout, begin by swirling Wicker White, Ivory White and Light Gray on your palette. Dip the dampened sponge into the swirled paint and turn the sponge in your hand before dipping it again onto the palette.

2 | Apply Painted Grout

Press the sponge onto the coaster to apply paint. Each time you lift the sponge, turn it (paint side down) in your hand to variegate the design. The harder you push onto the surface, the more subtle the design. The lighter you press, the more the design of the sponge will show through. Be sure to sponge the sides of the coasters as well. Set aside to dry.

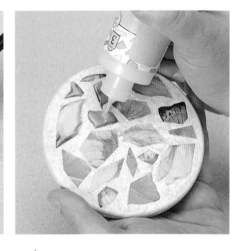

3 | Cut Tiles

Cut pieces of wallpaper into tiles appropriate for the size of the coaster into uneven shapes that emulate broken tile.

4 | Apply Adhesive

With the no. 12 flat, brush adhesive onto the surface. Work in a small area (about one-quarter the size of the coaster) so you can adhere the tiles before the glue dries.

5 | Place and Glaze Tiles

Because the wallpaper comes with adhesive on the back, you don't need to brush more glue on the back. Simply place the tiles on the surface and brush glue over them to secure. Let the adhesive dry completely before proceeding to glaze. To glaze the tiles, use the applicator bottle to outline slightly inside the edge of a tile, then fill in with glaze. The outline won't be necessary for smaller pieces. Apply a total of three coats of glaze to all tiles, allowing each to dry thoroughly to a clear finish before applying the next coat.

terrific terra-cotta pots

Plant pots are terrific candidates for faux mosaic surfaces because they are both useful and inexpensive. If you are apprehensive about trying a technique, a terra-cotta pot is a great place to try it because you don't have to worry about ruining an expensive surface. If you want to use the pots indoors, simply choose paint colors and wallpaper designs that match your décor.

MATERIALS

- terra-cotta pots, varying in size
- Light Periwinkle and Sunflower acrylic paint (FolkArt)
- gesso
- dragonfly wallpaper cutouts (Wallies pattern#12952)
- no. 1 flat and 2/0 liner brushes
- Tera Leigh Faux Mosaic Grout
- Tera Leigh Faux Mosaic Adhesive or other matte adhesive
- Tera Leigh Faux Mosaic Glaze or other thick dimensional glaze
- scissors
- palette
- water basin
- paper towels
- exterior gloss varnish

tip

When working with terra-cotta pots, use gesso instead of white paint. The terra cotta will show through acrylic paint, but gesso provides complete coverage. Do not, however, gesso the inside of the pot if you intend to fill it with a real plant—the gesso may be toxic to it. Instead, use a terra-cotta sealer available at craft and garden stores.

1 | Paint and Grout Pot

If your pot is dirty or rough, you can use a fine grit sanding paper to clean and smooth it before painting. Paint the bottom section of the pot with gesso using the no. 1 flat brush. Clean the brush and use it to paint the upper rim of the pot with Light Periwinkle.

Slip-slap faux grout on the bottom section with the no. 1 flat brush. Allow grout to dry completely.

2 | Cut Tiles

Cut the wallpaper into tiles appropriate for the size of the pot. The curved edges of the dragonfly wings will allow for some interesting shapes that re-create the appearance of cut china.

3 | Apply Adhesive

With the no. 1 flat, brush adhesive onto a small area of the pot. Work in an area no bigger than 3" (8cm) square. Place the tiles on the pot, then brush over them with adhesive using the no. 1 flat brush. Continue until the entire grouted portion of the pot is covered with tiles placed approximately ¼" (6mm) apart.

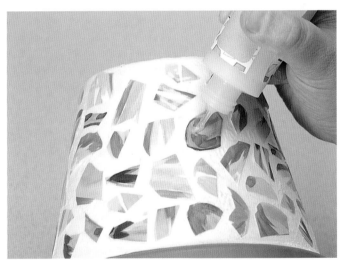

4 | Glaze Tiles

With the applicator bottle, outline slightly inside the edge of a tile, then fill in with glaze. Repeat for each tile on a small horizontal section of the pot. The wet glaze needs to dry level, so prop the pot so it doesn't drip. Allow glaze to dry thoroughly on each section before turning the pot. For the average size pot, you will want to glaze a section no larger than 1½" to 2" (4cm to 5cm) wide at a time. Once you have glazed all the way around the pot, apply two more coats of glaze in the same manner, allowing the second to dry before applying the third.

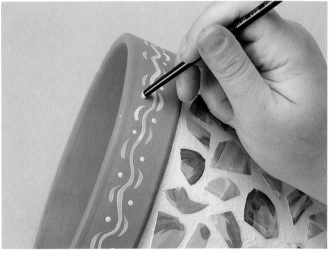

5 | Paint Wavy Lines

Once all the glaze is dry, you can embellish the pot with painted trim. With Sunflower paint thinned 40% with water, use a 2/0 liner brush to paint a wavy line in the center of the rim. Brace your hand when using a liner brush for best control. Paint short lines on top and below each curve of the wavy line. Dip the handle of the brush into the Sunflower and place a dot in each valley between the short lines to finish the embellishment. Dip into the paint before making each dot so each dot is the same size. For the best protection, varnish the painted rim with an exterior gloss varnish.

beauteous birdhouse

Birdhouses have been popular decorations—both indoor and out—for many years. The charming look of a birdhouse is a great way to bring the outdoors inside, as well as to spruce up your garden or patio. I love the colors in the rose designs featured in this piece. You might consider doing a matching tray or other pieces with a traditional decoupage to tie in the design colors as a group display.

MATERIALS

- birdhouse (Viking Woodcrafts)
- Light Periwinkle, Sunflower, Wicker White, Baby Pink, and Fresh Foliage acrylic paint (FolkArt)
- gesso, optional
- rose and leaves wallpaper cutouts (Wallies pattern #12106)
- no. 14 flat, ¾-inch (19mm) flat, no. 20 shader and no. 2 liner brushes
- Tera Leigh Faux Mosaic Grout
- Tera Leigh Faux Mosaic Tile Adhesive or other matte adhesive
- Tera Leigh Faux Mosaic Tile Glaze or other thick dimensional glaze
- scissors
- palette
- water basin
- paper towels
- outdoor sealer
- gloss varnish

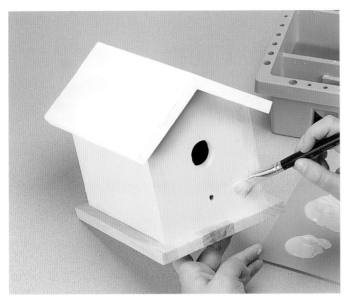

1 | Prepare and Paint Birdhouse

Sand and seal the entire birdhouse. Paint the roof with Wicker White or gesso using the ¾-inch (19mm) flat brush for the top of the roof, and the no. 14 flat brush for the edges.

Basecoat the sides of the birdhouse with Sunflower paint using the no. 20 shader brush. Complete coverage may require two coats of paint.

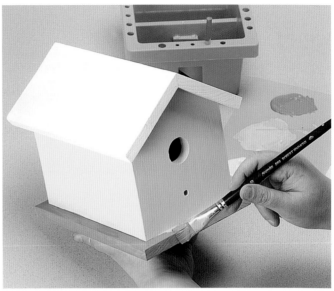

2 | Basecoat Base

Use the no. 20 shader brush and Light Periwinkle to paint the bottom and the horizontal base of the birdhouse.

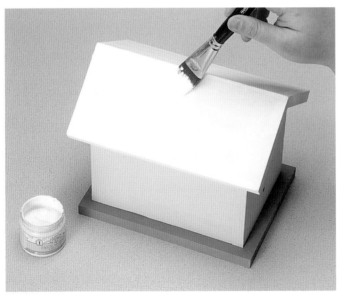

3 | Grout Roof

Spread faux grout on the roof of the birdhouse with the no. 20 shader brush, using the slip-slap technique. Allow grout to dry completely.

4 | Cut Tile

Cut pieces of wallpaper for the tiles on the birdhouse. For this project, I cut only a few tiles from the leaves to use as an accent color. The color scheme is primarily yellow and pink.

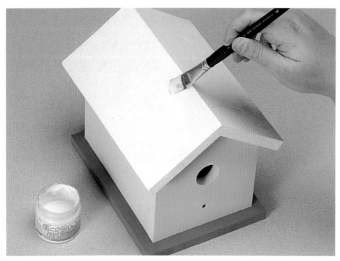

5 | Apply Adhesive

With the no. 20 shader, brush adhesive onto a small portion of the roof. Work in an area no bigger than 3" (8cm) square so the glue doesn't become too tacky to work over as you place the tiles.

6 | Place Tiles

Place the tiles on the roof approximately ¼" (6mm) apart, brushing over the top of the pieces with glue to keep them in place. Continue placing tiles until the grouted section is complete.

To gauge how much paper you will need for a specific surface, put a piece or pieces of paper over the area where the mosaic will be placed. If, for example, it takes one sheet of paper to cover the area and you will be using three designs, you know that you will need approximately one-third sheet of each design to create the mosaic. You should have a bit left over, which is a plus if you need to cut around a specific design.

7 | Paint Pink Wavy Lines

Using a no. 2 liner brush and Baby Pink thinned 40% with water, paint vertical wavy lines on the sides of the birdhouse. Eye the spacing, or measure if you prefer. I painted three lines on the narrow side of the birdhouse and four on the wider side. Spacing should be even but doesn't need to be exact. Whenever painting with a liner brush, brace your hand for best control.

8 | Paint White Wavy Lines

Clean the liner, then paint wavy lines on either side of the pink lines with Wicker White. Remember to brace your hand as you paint.

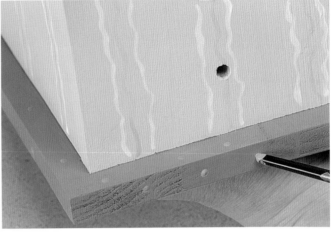

9 | Place Dots on Base

Add dots to the base by dipping the handle of your brush in Light Foliage Green paint, then pressing down on the base to create dots. Dip the handle in the paint before each dot to achieve dots of equal size. Paint the perch dowel Light Periwinkle using the no. 14 flat brush. When it's dry, insert it into the hole in the front of the birdhouse below the larger opening.

10 | Glaze Tiles

Prop the birdhouse so one side of the roof becomes level. With the applicator bottle, apply the glaze to the tiles, outlining each and filling them in. Complete all the tiles on one side of the roof and let dry completely before removing the prop. If the surface is not level, the glaze will drip off the tile or dry unevenly. Repeat the process for the other side of the roof. Apply two more coats of glaze, allowing each coat to dry completely before applying another coat, again propping the roof to keep it level. Varnish the painted parts of the birdhouse with gloss varnish. Use an exterior varnish if you'll be placing the piece outdoors.

tip

The more coats of glaze you apply, the more realistic the faux tile will appear in contrast to the grout. I suggest a minimum of three coats, but you may apply more or less if you like the look.

fabulous holiday mosaics

The holidays are always a wonderful time to explore your creativity. Whether you make these projects for your own house or for gifts, they will inspire you to make time to craft! As a twist, and to inspire you to think outside the box when looking for papers to use for your faux tile, I have used vintage Christmas cards as the tile for this chapter. If you are like me, you can't bear to throw away the beautiful cards you receive each year. Now you have the perfect excuse to save and use that stash of cards!

Faux Tiles

Old holiday cards are just one of many items you have around your house that could be used as faux tiles. Here are some other ideas:

ephemera from your travels (ticket stubs, receipts, business cards)

wrapping paper

greeting cards

old calendars

clip art books

photos or illustrations from old books destined for the trash bin

photographs scanned and printed on a laser printer, or copied on a copy machine

patterned tissue paper glued to cardstock

stickers or rub-on transfers on cardstock

handmade papers or mulberry paper (if it is thin, glue it to a like-colored sheet of cardstock for sturdiness)

old postage stamps

postcards

jewel-toned ornament

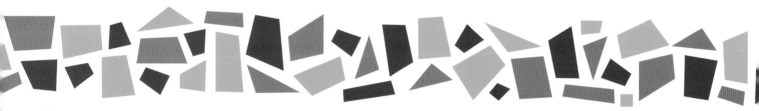

I chose these cards because of the beautiful colors represented in them. Because you are cutting the paper into small pieces, the actual design itself does not matter. However, unlike the abstract designs I have used in other chapters, I used focal point designs for both the projects in this chapter. This is similar to techniques used in traditional china and tile mosaics.

MATERIALS

- ceramic plaque/ornament (Cridgeware)

- Wicker White acrylic paint (FolkArt)

- vintage holiday cards

- no. 16 flat brush

- Tera Leigh Faux Mosaic Grout

- Tera Leigh Faux Mosaic Tile Adhesive or other matte adhesive

- Tera Leigh Faux Mosaic Tile Glaze or other thick dimensional glaze

- scissors

- palette

- water basin

- paper towels

1 | Apply Grout to Surface

This ceramic ornament does not require any preparation, except to ensure that it is clean and dust-free. Brush grout on the ornament with the no. 16 flat brush using a slip-slap motion. Let dry. If the background shows through, either apply a second coat of grout or paint over the grout with Wicker White paint using the no. 16 flat. Allow grout to dry well.

2 | Select Cards

Choose several cards to use for your mosaic. I used one of the poinsettias as the focus of this collage, cutting around it roughly as though it had been cut with tile nippers. I selected the other pieces primarily for their color in the background and cut them into smaller pieces.

3 | Apply Adhesive to Surface

With the same brush, apply adhesive to the center of the ornament for placement of the focal point. Here I used a poinsettia. Apply adhesive to the back of this piece and brush more adhesive over the top once it's in place.

4 | Place Smaller Tiles

Place smaller pieces of tile around the center. Work in small areas and brush adhesive onto the surface. Then apply adhesive to the back of the tile, brushing it over the top of the surface to adhere. Brush out any bubbles or excess glue.

5 | Glaze Tiles

Use the applicator bottle to outline and fill in each tile with glaze. Allow glaze to dry thoroughly. Apply two more coats of glaze, allowing the second to dry before applying the third.

retro-look memory book

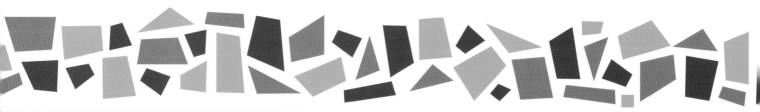

In the studio, as I created these pieces, the editor, photographer and I fell in love with a card with 1950s-looking characters inside ornaments. We decided that these would make a great focal point for the memory book collage. A mosaic with intact designs can have more than one focal point. I suggest laying out the design before you glue to make sure the layout is pleasing to you.

MATERIALS

- wood memory album cover, 6" x 9" (15cm x 23cm) (Walnut Hollow)

- Wicker White and Engine Red acrylic paint (FolkArt)

- gesso, optional

- vintage holiday cards

- no. 20 shader and ¾-inch (19mm) flat brushes

- Tera Leigh Faux Mosaic Grout

- Tera Leigh Faux Mosaic Tile Adhesive or other matte adhesive

- Tera Leigh Faux Mosaic Tile Glaze or other thick dimensional glaze

- scissors

- palette

- water basin

- paper towels

- gloss varnish

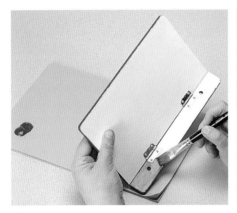

1 | Prep and Paint the Covers

Sand and seal the covers. Paint both sides of the back cover with Engine Red, then paint the inside and left edge of the front cover as well. Paint the main panel of the front cover with Wicker White or gesso. Use the ¾-inch (19mm) flat brush for painting the large areas and the no. 20 shader for the left edge. Several coats may be needed for full coverage.

2 | Select Cards

Choose several cards to use for your mosaic. I selected the card in the upper left and the text card for the main focus of the mosaic. I selected the others primarily for color since you won't be able to see the design once the cards are cut into tiles.

3 | Grout Cover

Apply grout on the front panel (white area) of the book using the slip-slap technique and the no. 20 shader brush. Allow the grout to dry completely.

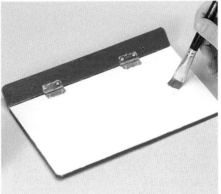

4 | Arrange Large Pieces

Use your scissors to cut out the words with uneven cuts, like it was nipped china. Cut pieces from the other cards into randomly shaped tiles. Arrange the focal pieces on the surface to determine the best positioning before you glue them down.

5 | Apply Adhesive

With the no. 20 shader, brush adhesive onto the area in which you'll be placing the words. If you have a large piece for the focus of your mosaic, always place that first, then place smaller pieces around it. If you are comfortable with the design, remove the pieces, then glue into place. If not, just lift each piece and glue it as you go.

6 | Adhere and Glaze Tiles

Apply adhesive and glue the words and focal pieces in place. Then apply adhesive to a small area of the surface and fill in around the design with smaller pieces of tile. To glaze, use the applicator bottle to outline slightly inside the edge of a tile, then fill in with glaze. Repeat on all tiles. Allow glaze to dry, then apply two more coats, allowing each to dry.

Use a no. 20 shader to varnish the areas of painted wood.

resources

You'll find most of the materials in local craft or art supply stores. Most independent stores will order product for you if you need something they don't have.

If you cannot find the product locally, I have provided the manufacturer information for each of the products used in the book. They can provide vendor information, and some of the manufacturers listed sell directly from their sites.

Surfaces

Cridge Inc.
CridgeWare Division
101 Lower Morrisville Road
Fallsington, PA 19054
215-295-2797 ext. 727
www.cridgeware.com
ceramic coasters (CW113), ceramic
plaque (CW306)

Hygloss Products, Inc.
45 Hathaway Street
Wallington, NJ 07057
800-444-9456
www.hygloss.com
wood drawer pull

Viking Woodcrafts
1317 8th Street SE
Waseca, MN 56093
800-328-0116
www.vikingwoodcrafts.com
hand mirror (20-9462), jewelry box (20-9943), pine triangular box (102-9063), tissue box (200-0063), soap dispenser box (09-1284), tray (20-9555), crate/rectangle box (20-10276), candlesticks (15-6512), napkin rings (16-1081), scalloped rim plate (18-1709), wooden lamp (102-9041), birdhouse cloud cabin (24-1106)

Walnut Hollow Farm, Inc.
1409 State Road 23
Dodgeville, WI 53533
800-950-5101
www.walnuthollow.com
wooden ball knobs, scallop frame (23420), small open base pendulum clock (23022), small pendulum clock movement (TQ810P), contemporary memory album cover (3704)

Western Woodworks
1142 Olive Branch Lane
San Jose, CA 05120
408-997-2356
www.westernwoodworks.com
key rings, clock pendants

General Supplies and Materials

Anna Griffin Incorporated
733 Lambert Drive
Atlanta, Georgia 30324
404-817-8170
www.annagriffin.com
Anna Griffin decorative papers

Daler-Rowney USA
2 Corporate Drive
Cranbury, New Jersey 08512-9584
609-655-5252
www.daler-rowney.com
Robert Simmons Sapphire Brushes, brush basin, Cryla white gesso primer

DMD Industries, Inc.
2300 S. Old Missouri Road
Springdale, AR 72764
800-805-9890
www.dmdind.com
cardstock paper packs

Houston Art, Inc.
10770 Moss Ridge Road
Houston, TX 77043-1175
800-272-3804
www.houstonart.com
Athena gray palette, Mona Lisa Metal Leaf Adhesive Spray, Mona Lisa Metal Leaf in 23-Karat Gold, Bronze, Silver

The McCall Pattern Company
P.O. Box 3100
Manhattan, KS 66505-3100
800-255-2762 ext. 485
www.wallies.com
Wallies wallpaper cutouts

Plaid Enterprises
P.O. Box 7600
Norcross, GA 30091-7600
800-842-4197
www.plaidonline.com
FolkArt paints, outdoor sealer and varnish, All Night Media rubber stamps

Colorbök, Inc.
2716 Baker Rd
Dexter, MI 48130
800-366-4660
www.tracyporter.com/make_and_create/index.shtml
Tracy Porter scrapbook papers

Ranger Industries, Inc.
15 Park Road
Tinton Falls, NJ 17724
800-244-2211
www.rangerink.com
Tera Leigh Faux Mosaic Grout, Tile Adhesive and Tile Glaze

Wolff Industries, Inc.
107 Interstate Park
Spartanburg, SC 29303
800-888-3832
www.wolffind.com
Kai scissors

Overseas Resources

www.artdiscount.co.uk (UK)
www.currys.com (Canada)
www.folkart.net (Canada)
www.lawrence.co.uk (UK)
www.theartshop.com.au (Australia)
www.uniqueimpressions.com.au (Australia)

index

Get creative with North Light Books!

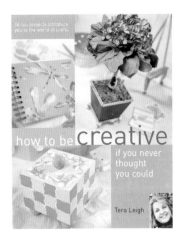

How to Be Creative If You Never Thought You Could

Author and artist Tera Leigh makes it easy for readers to discover their creative spirit. She defines exactly what creativity is and how our creative ability can be realized through the fantastic world of crafts. You'll find 16 fun and easy-to-make projects that enable you to explore a wide variety of craft media and techniques as well as valuable tips, exercises and affirmations for overcoming obstacles in your creativity. Named to the "Top Ten Craft & Hobby Books" list by the American Library Association.

ISBN 1-58180-293-5, paperback, 128 pages, #32170-K

Inspired by the Garden

Inspired by the Garden presents 16 garden-inspired projects for inside and out. Using a range of crafting techniques and materials, this book showcases fun yet sophisticated garden décor projects perfect for crafters of all skill levels. Featuring popular garden motifs, projects include mosaic garden tables, matching pots and watering can, cards made with pressed flowers, a garden apron and more!

ISBN 1-58180-434-2, paperback, 128 pages, #32630-K

Brilliant Stained Glass Mosaics

Create stunning, sophisticated designs for both home and garden décor with easy mosaic techniques. Combining traditional opaque mosaics and stained glass, you'll discover exciting glass-on-glass mosaic projects come to life when illuminated by candlelight, incandescent or natural light. There are 12 projects in all, including windows, vases, candleholders, picture frames, light fixtures and more!

ISBN 1-58180-185-8, paperback, 128 pages, #31955-K

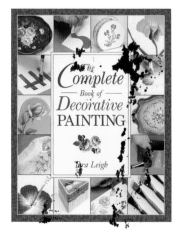

The Complete Book of Decorative Painting

This book is the must-have one-stop reference for decorative painters, crafters, home decorators and do-it-yourselfers. It's packed with solutions to every painting challenge, including surface preparation, lettering, borders, faux finishes, strokework techniques and more! You'll also find five fun-to-paint projects designed to instruct, challenge and entertain you—no matter what your skill level.

ISBN 1-58180-062-2, paperback, 256 pages, #31803-K

These books and other fine North Light titles are available from your local art & craft retailer, bookstore, online supplier or by calling 1-800-448-0915.